creating
success

How to Manage People

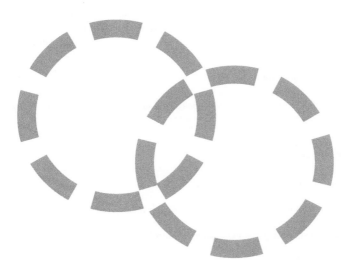

Michael Armstrong

KoganPage

LONDON PHILADELPHIA NEW DELHI

Publisher's note

Every possible effort has been made to ensure that the information contained in this book is accurate at the time of going to press, and the publishers and authors cannot accept responsibility for any errors or omissions, however caused. No responsibility for loss or damage occasioned to any person acting, or refraining from action, as a result of the material in this publication can be accepted by the editor, the publisher or the author.

First published in Great Britain and the United States in 2008 by Kogan Page Limited
Second edition published 2013
Third edition published 2016

2nd Floor, 45 Gee Street	1518 Walnut Street, Suite 900	4737/23 Ansari Road
London	Philadelphia PA 19102	Daryaganj
EC1V 3RS	USA	New Delhi 110002
United Kingdom		India

© Michael Armstrong, 2008, 2013, 2016

ISBN   978 0 7494 7567 3
E-ISBN   978 0 7494 7568 0

British Library Cataloguing-in-Publication Data

A CIP record for this book is available from the British Library.

Library of Congress Cataloging-in-Publication Control Number

LCCN: 2016017788

Typeset by Graphicraft Limited, Hong Kong
Print production managed by Jellyfish
Printed and bound by Ashford Colour Press Ltd.

Contents

Contents

Preface

The aim of this book is to give practical advice to managers and team leaders on how to manage the people in their teams – getting the best results from them and dealing with any problems that may arise.

The book focuses on what front-line managers, ie those directly controlling teams of people, have to do themselves. A business may have all sorts of progressive human resource (HR) policies but it is managers who bring them to life. Many managers have to do their job without HR advice and this book is particularly designed to meet their needs.

The 17 exercises in this book are designed to test understanding and to explore issues in greater depth. The appendix contains notes on each exercise.

1 Managing people – what managers do

Managers get things done through people. They depend on their wholehearted commitment and support. Gaining this commitment and support, motivating and engaging people and ensuring that they know what they are expected to do and how to do it is down to line managers. And it is a difficult task requiring a range of demanding skills.

The importance of the task is increased because so far as many people are concerned, their manager is the organization. They do not have much contact with other people in authority. That is why it is said that people leave their managers, not their organization.

Managers have to treat people right, that is, fairly and with respect and consideration. But managers are there to achieve the task; they must also see that the members of their team understand what they are expected to do and then do it. This means they have to exercise leadership, motivate their staff and enhance their engagement. They have to ensure that people with the right skills are in the right jobs and that they perform well in exercising their skills in those jobs.

But managing people is not always easy. There will be problems when there is conflict, when people do not perform well, and when their behaviour is unacceptable. Managers have to deal with these people problems. The organization may have capability and disciplinary procedures but it is managers who implement them.

EXERCISE 1.1

Management qualities
What do you think are the most important qualities a manager should possess?

SUMMARY POINTS

Managers:

- get things done through people;
- have to treat people right; that is, fairly and with respect and consideration;
- have to exercise leadership, motivate their staff and enhance their engagement.

2 Treat people right

Treating people right means treating them fairly and with respect. But it is not about going soft on them. It is necessary to be firm as well as fair, to set standards and to ensure that they are met. Ed Lawler, a leading American management expert, wrote that 'Treating people right is a fundamental key to creating organizational effectiveness'. He also noted that the concept of treating people right recognizes the fact that 'Both organizations and individuals need to succeed. One cannot succeed without the other' (Lawler, 2003).

The seven principles of treating people right are:

1 Treat people with respect.
2 Treat people fairly.
3 Create the right work environment.
4 Help people to develop their capabilities and skills.
5 Provide leadership.
6 Get to know team members.
7 Define expectations and ensure they are met.

Treat people with respect

To respect someone is to recognize their qualities, ensuring that they feel valued and treating them with dignity and courtesy – no belittling, no bullying. It means being sensitive to the differences between people, taking this diversity into account in any dealings with them. It involves honouring their contribution and listening to what they have to say. It also means recognizing that people may have legitimate grievances and responding to them promptly, fully and sympathetically.

Treat people fairly

Treating people fairly means that you should:

- give proper consideration to their views and circumstances;
- apply policies and decisions consistently to all concerned;
- provide adequate explanations of decisions made (transparency);
- avoid personal bias with regard to individuals or categories of people (no favouritism);
- ensure that people are rewarded equitably in comparison with others in the organization in accordance with their contribution;
- see that people get what was promised to them (deliver the deal);
- define the standards people are expected to achieve;
- indicate clearly to people where you believe that the defined standards are not being reached and give them a chance to improve.

Create the right work environment

People should feel that their work is worthwhile. Their jobs should make good use of their skills and abilities and as far as possible provide some autonomy so that they have a reasonable degree of control over their activities and decisions.

Employees also need feedback – information about how well they are doing, preferably obtained for themselves from their work rather than from their manager. As described in Chapter 4, these are all factors that, if they are present in jobs, will increase intrinsic motivation – motivation from the work itself. They can be considerably influenced by the ways in which work is organized – the design of the work system.

The fundamental requirement is for the work system to operate efficiently and flexibly. It is necessary to provide for the smooth flow of processes and activities and ensure that resources – people, materials, plant, equipment and money – are used effectively. But in designing or managing a work system it is also necessary to consider what needs to be done to treat people right. The system should enable employees to gain fulfilment from their work by as far as possible allowing scope for variety, challenge and autonomy. It should provide a good environment in terms of working conditions and a healthy and safe system of work, bearing in mind the need to minimize stress and pay attention to ergonomic considerations in the design of equipment and work stations.

Help people to develop their capabilities and skills

It is in your own interest and that of your organization to enhance the skills and capabilities of the people you manage through coaching, training and, importantly, giving them scope to learn or develop skills by providing new work opportunities or challenges. In doing so you will be 'treating them right'. They will be equipped with the means to gain greater fulfilment from their work by achieving more in their existing jobs and by obtaining the experience and skills which will further their careers.

Furthering development means noticing when formal training experiences or opportunities for on-the-job training can help someone. You should give your people time and space to learn new skills.

Your role as a coach is particularly important. Every time you give somebody a new task to do you are creating a learning opportunity.

Provide leadership

Leadership is about treating people right. It helps them by giving a sense of direction and by providing support when necessary. Effective leadership means that people know where they are going and are guided on how to get there.

Get to know team members

You can't treat individual members of your team right unless you get to know them. You need to know their strengths and weaknesses, their ambitions and their concerns about work. Performance management systems that provide for regular review meetings between managers and their staff can help to do this. But it should be an everyday affair. The more you are in contact with your people the better you will get to know them. It's no good hiding in your office or behind a desk. You have to get out and talk to people. It's called management by walking about, and it's one of the best ways of building good relationships.

Define expectations and ensure they are met

You treat people right when you make sure that they understand and accept what is expected of them – standards of performance and behaviour. You need to clarify roles, what has to be achieved and how it is to be achieved. And this should be a matter for mutual agreement. You are not there as a manager simply to order people around. You want willing cooperation, not grudging submission.

But you have to ensure that the standards are met. If they are not, this is when you need to be firm. Treating people right is not about being soft with them. It is right to take a firm line if someone under-performs without good reason or misbehaves.

You also have to remember that you have to earn the respect of your team members.

TEN WAYS OF GAINING RESPECT

1 Get things done well – impress people with your achievements.

2 Be professional; this means applying expertise in carrying out your work and acting responsibly at all times.

3 Engender trust – the firm belief that you can be relied on.

4 Respond promptly to requests for help or information.

5 Behave in a friendly and approachable manner.

6 Act firmly and with integrity, displaying honesty, probity, sincerity, fairness and morality.

7 Be polite, persistent and persuasive.

8 Deal calmly with people – never lose your temper.

9 Listen to people.

10 Take time to say thank you.

EXERCISE 2.1

Treating people with respect
What is involved in treating people with respect?

SUMMARY POINTS

- Treating people right means treating them fairly and with respect, amongst other things. But it is not about going soft on them. It is necessary to be firm as well as fair.
- The seven principles of treating people right are:
  1 Treat people fairly.
  2 Treat people with respect.
  3 Create the right work environment.
  4 Help people to develop their capabilities and skills.
  5 Provide leadership.
  6 Get to know team members.
  7 Define expectations and ensure they are met.

3 Leadership

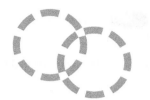

As a manager of people, your role is to ensure that the members of your team give their best to achieve the result you want. In other words you are a leader – you set the direction and ensure that people follow you.

Leadership is the process of developing and communicating a vision for the future, motivating and guiding people and securing their engagement. Leaders know where they want to go and make sure that everyone in their teams goes in the same direction.

According to Margaret Thatcher leadership is telling people what to do and then making them do it. This sort of autocratic approach may have been all very well for Thatcher in her heyday but it didn't work in the end. People do not like being coerced. It is preferable to regard a leader as someone who takes people where they want to go, while a great leader takes people where they don't necessarily want to go but ought to be.

To be an effective leader you need to:

- know what leaders do;
- be aware of the different styles of leadership;
- appreciate the qualities that make a good leader;
- learn from examples of effective leaders;
- understand the reality of leadership;
- know how best to develop your leadership abilities.

What leaders do

The most convincing analysis of what leaders do was produced by John Adair (1973). He explained the three essential roles of leaders:

1 Define the task – make it quite clear what the group is expected to do.

2 Achieve the task – that is why the group exists. Leaders ensure that the group's purpose is fulfilled. If it is not, the result is frustration, disharmony, criticism and, eventually perhaps, disintegration of the group.

3 Maintain effective relationships – between themselves and the members of the group, and between the people within the group. These relationships are effective if they contribute to achieving the task. They can be divided into those concerned with the team and its morale and sense of common purpose, and those concerned with individuals and how they are motivated.

Adair suggested that demands on leaders are best expressed as three areas of need which they must satisfy. These are: (1) task needs – to get the job done, (2) individual needs – to harmonize the needs of the individual with the needs of the task and the group and (3) group maintenance needs – to build and maintain team spirit. As shown in Figure 3.1, he modelled these demands as three interlocking circles.

This model indicates that the task, individual and group needs are interdependent. Satisfying task needs will also satisfy group and individual needs. Task needs, however, cannot be met unless attention is paid to individual and group needs, and looking after individual needs will also contribute to satisfying group needs and vice versa. There is a risk of becoming so task orientated that leaders ignore individual and group or team needs. It is just as dangerous to be too people orientated, focusing on meeting individual or group needs at the expense of the task. The best leaders are those who keep these three needs satisfied and in balance according to the demands of the situation.

FIGURE 3.1 John Adair's model of what leaders do

Leadership styles

Leadership style is the approach managers use in exercising leadership, and is sometimes called management style. There are many styles of leadership. To greater or lesser degrees, leaders can adopt any one of the styles described in Figure 3.2.

It should not be assumed that any one style is right in any circumstances. And there may be intermediate points between the extremes shown in Figure 3.2. There is no such thing as an ideal leadership style. It all depends. The factors affecting the degree to which a style is appropriate will be the type of organization, the nature of the task, the characteristics of the individuals in the leader's team and of the group as a whole and, importantly, the personality of the leader.

Effective leaders are capable of flexing their style to meet the demands of the situation. Normally democratic leaders may have to shift into more of a directive mode when faced with a crisis, but they make clear what they are doing and why. Poor leaders change their style arbitrarily so that their team members are confused and do not know what to expect next.

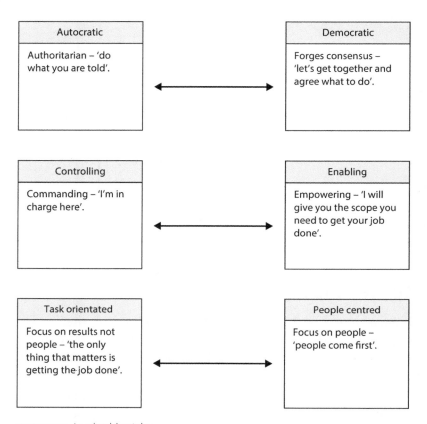

Autocratic	Democratic
Authoritarian – 'do what you are told'.	Forges consensus – 'let's get together and agree what to do'.

Controlling	Enabling
Commanding – 'I'm in charge here'.	Empowering – 'I will give you the scope you need to get your job done'.

Task orientated	People centred
Focus on results not people – 'the only thing that matters is getting the job done'.	Focus on people – 'people come first'.

FIGURE 3.2 Leadership styles

Good leaders may also flex their style when dealing with individual team members according to their characteristics. Some people need more positive direction than others. Others respond best if they are involved in decision making with their boss. But there is a limit to the degree of flexibility that should be used. It is unwise to differentiate too much between the ways in which individuals are treated or to be inconsistent in one's approach.

What makes a good leader?

What makes a good leader? There is no universal answer to this question. But Lao-Tzu in the 6th century BCE had a pretty good stab at it:

> *A leader is best*
> *When people barely know that he exists.*
> *Not so good when people obey and acclaim him.*
> *Worst when they despise him.*
> *Fail to honour people, they fail to honour you.*
> *But a good leader who talks little,*
> *When his work is done, his aim fulfilled,*
> *They will all say, 'We did this ourselves'.*

Effective leaders are confident and know what they need to do. They have the ability to take charge, convey their vision to their team, get their team members into action and ensure that they achieve their agreed goals. They are trustworthy, effective at influencing people and earn the respect of their team. They are aware of their own strengths and weaknesses and are skilled at understanding what will motivate their team members. They appreciate the advantages of consulting and involving people in decision making. They can switch flexibly from one leadership style to another to meet the demands of different situations and people.

One of the key skills a leader or manager needs is an ability to analyse and read situations and to establish order and clarity in situations of ambiguity. Leaders need to have a sense of purpose, and an ability to influence others, interpret situations, negotiate and express their views, often in the face of opposition.

Research conducted recently by the Work Foundation (Tamkin *et al*, 2010) involving 260 in-depth interviews conducted with 77 business leaders from six high-profile organizations found that outstanding leaders:

- viewed things as a whole rather than compartmentalizing them;
- connect the parts through a guiding sense of purpose;
- are highly motivated to achieve excellence and are focused on organizational outcomes, vision and purpose;
- understand they cannot create performance themselves but are conduits for performance through their influence on others;
- watch themselves carefully and act consistently to achieve excellence through their interactions and their embodiment of the leadership role.

How do successful leaders do it?

Here are three examples.

Herb Kelleber – CEO, Southwest Airlines

Southwest Airlines is generally regarded as the world's most successful airline. It grew at a nearly constant annual rate of 10–15 per cent over its first 32 years of existence under the leadership of Herb Kelleber. He was described by *Fortune Magazine* as 'perhaps the best CEO in America'.

As a leader, Herb Kelleber focused on relationships based on shared goals, shared knowledge and mutual respect. His theme was that tasks are achieved through the goodwill and support of others.

This goodwill and support originates in the leader seeing people as people, not just another resource for use in getting results. He expanded this as follows:

- Take the organizational pyramid.
- Turn it upside down on its point. Down here, at the bottom, you've got the people at headquarters. Up there, at the top, you've got the people who are out there in the field, on the front lines.
- They're the ones that make things happen, not us.

Bill George – Chairman and CEO of Medtronic (the biomedical engineering company)

Under his 12-year leadership the market capitalization of Medtronic, increased at the rate of 35 per cent per year from $1.1 billion to $60 billion.

He attributed this to what he called the practice of authentic leadership which he defined as follows:

- authentic leaders genuinely want to serve others through their leadership;
- they are more interested in empowering the people they lead to make a difference than they are in power, money or prestige for themselves;
- they lead with purpose, meaning and values;
- they build enduring relationships with people;
- others follow them because they know where they stand;
- they are consistent and self-disciplined.

Jack Welch – Chief Executive of General Electric

Jack Welch wrote that for a leader:

- success is all about growing others;
- it's about making the people who work for you smarter, bigger and bolder;
- nothing you do as an individual matters, except how you nurture and support your team and increase their self-confidence;
- your success as a leader will come not from what you do, but from the reflected glory of your team.

The reality of leadership

The reality of leadership is that many first line managers and supervisors are appointed or promoted to their posts with some idea, possibly, of what their managerial or supervisory duties are, but with no appreciation of the leadership skills they need. They see their role as being to tell people what to do and then make sure that they do it. They may focus on getting the job done and neglect everything else.

However, the better ones will rely on their know-how (authority goes to the person who knows), their quiet confidence and their cool, analytical approach to dealing with problems. Any newly appointed leader or individual who is progressing to a higher level of leadership will benefit from a leadership development programme which will help them to understand and apply the skills they need.

Leadership checklists

Task

- What needs to be done and why?
- What results have to be achieved and by when?
- What problems have to be overcome?
- To what extent are these problems straightforward?
- Is there a crisis situation?
- What has to be done now to deal with the crisis?
- What are these priorities?
- What pressures are likely to be exerted?

Individuals

- What are their strengths and weaknesses?
- What are likely to be the best ways of motivating them?

- What tasks are they best at doing?
- Is there scope to increase flexibility by developing new skills?
- How well do they perform in achieving targets and performance standards?
- To what extent can they manage their own performance and development?
- Are there any areas where there is a need to develop skill or competence?
- How can I provide them with the sort of support and guidance that will improve their performance?

Teams

- How well is the team organized?
- Does the team work well together?
- How can the commitment and motivation of the team be achieved?
- What is the team good and not so good at doing?
- What can I do to improve the performance of the team?
- Are team members flexible – capable of carrying out different tasks?
- To what extent can the team manage its own performance?
- Is there scope to empower the team so that it can take on greater responsibility for setting standards, monitoring performance and taking corrective action?
- Can the team be encouraged to work together to produce ideas for improving performance?

A 10-POINT PLAN FOR DEVELOPING LEADERSHIP SKILLS

1 Understand what is meant by leadership.

2 Appreciate the different leadership styles available.

3 Assess what you believe to be your fundamental leadership style.

4 Get other people, colleagues and indeed your own team members, to tell you what they think your leadership style is and how well it works.

5 In the light of this information, consider what you need to do and can do to modify your style, bearing in mind that you have to go on being the same person. In other words, your style should still be a natural one.

6 Think about the typical situations and problems with which you are confronted as a leader. Will your leadership style, modified as necessary, be appropriate for all of them? If not, can you think of any of those situations where a different style would have been better? If so, think about what you need to do to be able to flex your style as necessary without appearing to be inconsistent to your team.

7 Examine the various explanations of the qualities that make a good leader and assess your own performance using the questionnaire set out below. Decide what you need to do – what you can do – about any weaknesses.

8 Think about or observe any managers you know whom you have worked for or with.

9 Assess each of them in terms of the qualities set out in the leadership skills questionnaire above.

10 Consider what you can learn from them about effective and less effective leadership behaviours. In the light of this, assess where you could usefully modify your own leadership behaviours.

EXERCISE 3.1

Assess your leadership skills

Assess your own leadership skills by completing the questionnaire below. You should be as frank as possible with yourself. Note your strengths and weaknesses and decide how you can make the best use of the former and overcome the latter.

The questionnaire could also be used by your team members to assess you – well worthwhile but it takes quite a lot of courage and determination to do it. You could even use it to assess your own boss but you would have to be sure that he or she can take constructive criticisms.

Circle the number which most closely matches your opinion

LEADERSHIP BEHAVIOUR	STRONGLY AGREE	AGREE	DISAGREE	STRONGLY DISAGREE
1 Makes clear to people what they have to do and achieve	4	3	2	1
2 Consistently gets good results	4	3	2	1
3 Encourages people to use their own initiative	4	3	2	1
4 Gives people sufficient scope to do their job	4	3	2	1
5 Gives people the guidance, coaching and support they need to do a good job	4	3	2	1
6 Gives regular feedback to people on their performance	4	3	2	1
7 Values the opinions of team members	4	3	2	1
8 Recognizes the achievements of the team and its individual members	4	3	2	1
9 Treats people with respect	4	3	2	1
10 Treats people fairly	4	3	2	1

SUMMARY POINTS

- Leadership is the process of developing and communicating a vision for the future, motivating and guiding people and securing their engagement.

- The three essential roles of leaders are to define the task, achieve the task and maintain effective relationships – between themselves and the members of the group, and between the people within the group.

- Leadership style is the approach managers use in exercising leadership. The main types of styles are autocratic or democratic, controlling or enabling, and task orientated or people centred.

- Effective leaders are confident and know what they need to do. They have the ability to take charge, convey their vision to their team, encourage their team members into action and ensure that they achieve their agreed goals.

4 Motivating people

Motivation is the process of getting people to move in the direction you want them to go. It is therefore very much a part of leadership, which is about spurring people into action and ensuring that they continue taking that action in order to achieve the required results.

While your organization can help to motivate people through its reward policies and practices (its reward systems such as performance pay), as a manager you still have a major part to play by deploying your own motivating skills to ensure that people give their best. You cannot rely upon your organization to do it for you. As the person in day-to-day contact with employees you are in the strongest position to motivate them.

Remember that people often have a choice about how they carry out their work and how hard they work. This is sometimes called their 'discretionary effort'. It can make the difference between simply doing a job and doing a great job. Your role as a motivator is to obtain the maximum amount of discretionary effort from the members of your team.

Unfortunately, approaches to motivation are too often underpinned by simplistic assumptions about how it works. The process of motivation is much more complex than many people believe and motivational practices are most likely to function well if they are based on proper understanding of what is involved.

This chapter therefore:

- defines motivation;
- explains the basic process of motivation;
- describes the two types of motivation – intrinsic and extrinsic;
- explores in greater depth the various theories of motivation which explain and amplify the basic process;
- examines the practical implications of the motivation theories.

What follows is based on the huge amount of practical research that has provided the basis for the development of motivation theory. But don't let the word 'theory' put you off. It has been said that 'there is nothing so practical as a good theory'. This means that theories based on extensive research in the field, ie within organizations, such as those concerned with goals and expectations described later in this chapter, can reveal what approaches work best and how to put them into practice.

Motivation defined

A motive is a reason for doing something. Motivation is concerned with the factors that influence people to behave in certain ways. The three components of motivation are:

- direction – what a person is trying to do;
- effort – how hard a person is trying;
- persistence – how long a person keeps on trying.

Motivation can be described as goal-directed behaviour. Well-motivated people are those with clearly defined goals who take action which they expect will achieve those goals. Such people may be self-motivated, and as long as this means they are going in the right direction to achieve what they are there to achieve, then this is the best form of motivation. But you cannot rely on it. Most people need to be motivated to a greater or lesser degree.

The process of motivation

Motivation is initiated by the conscious or unconscious recognition of an unsatisfied need. A goal is then established which it is believed will satisfy this need and a decision is made on the action that is expected will achieve the goal. If the goal is achieved the need will be satisfied and the behaviour is likely to be repeated the next time a similar need emerges. If the goal is not achieved the same action is less likely to be repeated. This process is modelled in Figure 4.1 below:

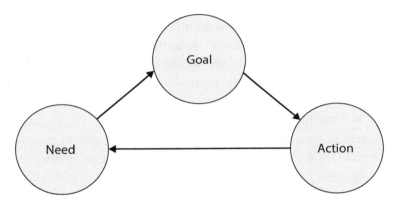

FIGURE 4.1 The process of motivation

This model illustrates a process of motivation, which involves setting goals that are likely to meet individual needs and encouraging the behaviour required to achieve those goals. But it is necessary to remember two fundamental truths about motivation. The first is that there is a multiplicity of needs, goals and actions which depend on the person and the situation. It is unwise to assume that any one approach to motivation will appeal to all affected by it. Motivation policies and practices must recognize that people are different. Second, while we can observe how people behave – the actions they take – we cannot be certain about what has motivated them to behave that way, ie what the needs and goals were that have affected their actions. These factors mean that simplistic methods of increasing motivation such as performance pay rarely work as well as intended.

Types of motivation

There are two types of motivation:

1 *Intrinsic motivation* – this takes place when the work someone does is personally rewarding, ie motivation by the work itself. It implies that work can be carried out for its own sake as a worthwhile activity rather than to get an external reward. The factors that make work intrinsically rewarding are an interesting and challenging job, responsibility (feeling that the work is important and having control over one's own resources), autonomy (freedom to act), scope to use and develop skills and abilities, and opportunities for advancement.

2 *Extrinsic motivation* – what is done to or for people to motivate them. This includes financial rewards, recognition (praise) and promotion. Punishments such as disciplinary action, withholding pay or criticism can be seen as extrinsic motivators but this is a negative approach which is seldom, if ever, effective in the longer term.

Extrinsic motivators can have an immediate and strong effect, but it will not necessarily last long. The intrinsic motivators, which are concerned with the 'quality of working life', are likely to make a deeper and longer-term impact. This is because they are inherent in the work and the work environment and are not imposed from outside. Managers can exert considerable influence on that work environment and this can be a powerful motivational tool. Some commentators such as Daniel Pink claim that only intrinsic motivation is effective and that extrinsic motivators such as financial incentives never work. But while intrinsic motivation is clearly crucial, to suggest that financial rewards are always useless is far too sweeping a statement. They can be effective if they are appropriate for the type of work or person involved and if they are properly designed and managed. And the recognition of achievements can be a potent motivator.

Motivation theories

The process of motivation as described above is broadly based on a number of motivation theories, which attempt to explain in more detail what it is all about. These theories have proliferated over the years. Some of them, like the crude 'carrot and stick' approach to motivation, which states that people can only be motivated to work by rewards and punishments, have been discredited, although they still underpin the beliefs of some managers about motivation. The following powerful attack on the carrot and stick method of motivation was offered by Daniel Pink in his best-selling book, *Drive* (2011).

THE VIEWS OF DANIEL PINK ON WHAT IS WRONG WITH THE CARROT AND STICK METHOD OF MOTIVATION

At the heart of the carrot and stick approach are two elegant and simple ideas:

Rewarding an activity will get you more of it.
Punishing an activity will get you less of it.

Carrots and sticks can produce precisely the opposite of their intended aims. Methods designed to increase motivation can dampen it. Actions aimed at increasing creativity can reduce it. Programmes to promote good deeds can make them disappear; meanwhile, instead of restraining negative behaviour, rewards and punishments can often set it loose – and give rise to cheating, addiction, and desperately myopic thinking.

Other theories such as those developed by Maslow and Herzberg are no longer highly regarded because they are not supported by field research (Maslow, 1954) or because the field research was flawed (Herzberg, 1966). However, Maslow, did contribute the useful notions that 'man (sic) is a wanting animal' and that 'a satisfied want is no longer a motivator'. And Herzberg convincingly argued that extrinsic motivation, especially money, was a 'hygiene factor', which will not provide lasting satisfaction but could cause dissatisfaction if the organization gets it wrong. Conversely, he noted, intrinsic motivation – 'motivation through the work itself' – was a 'satisfier', which could make a long-term positive impact on performance. Both these writers together with others in the field developed classifications of the various needs that can motivate people, such as achievement, responsibility, autonomy and growth.

The two most significant motivation theories for the practitioner are goal theory and expectancy theory.

Goal theory

Goal theory states that motivation and performance are higher when individuals are set specific goals, when goals are difficult but accepted, and when there is feedback on performance. Participation in goal setting is important as a means of getting agreement to the setting of higher goals. Difficult goals must be agreed and their achievement reinforced by guidance and advice. As long as they are agreed, demanding goals lead to better performance than easy ones. Finally, feedback is vital in maintaining motivation, particularly towards the achievement of even higher goals.

Expectancy theory

Expectancy theory states that people will be motivated when a clearly perceived and usable relationship exists between performance and outcome, and the outcome is seen as a means of satisfying needs. In other words they (1) are clear about the goals they are aiming for,

(2) believe in their ability to reach those goals, (3) are aware of the rewards they will get from achieving the goals, and (4) consider that the rewards will be worth the effort involved.

Expectancy theory explains why extrinsic financial motivation – for example, an incentive or bonus scheme – works only if the link between effort and reward is clear and the reward is worth having, ie there is a clear line of sight between them. It also explains why intrinsic motivation arising from the work itself can be more powerful than extrinsic motivation. Intrinsic motivation outcomes are more under the control of individuals, who can place greater reliance on their past experiences to indicate the extent to which positive and advantageous results are likely to be obtained by their behaviour.

This theory was developed by Porter and Lawler into a model which suggests that the two basic factors determining the effort people put into their jobs are first, the value of the rewards to individuals in so far as they satisfy their needs for security, social esteem, autonomy, and growth, and second, the probability that rewards depend on effort, as perceived by individuals – in other words, their expectations about the relationships between effort and reward (Porter and Lawler, 1968). This means that the greater the value of a set of rewards and the higher the probability that receiving each of these rewards depends upon effort, the greater the effort that will be put forth in a given situation.

But mere effort is not enough. It has to be effective effort if it is to produce the desired performance. The two variables in addition to effort which affect achievement are:

- Ability – individual characteristics such as intelligence, skills and know-how.
- Role perceptions – what individuals want to do or think they are required to do. These are good from the viewpoint of the organization if they correspond with what it thinks the individual ought to be doing. They are poor if the views of the individual and the organization do not coincide.

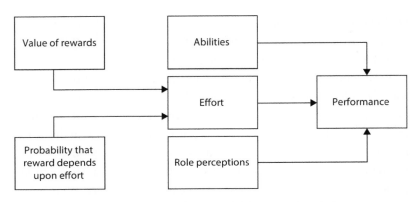

FIGURE 4.2 Motivation expectancy theory model (Porter and Lawler)

A model of expectancy theory, which incorporates these factors, is shown in Figure 4.2.

The key messages of motivation theory

The key messages provided by motivation theory are summarized below.

Extrinsic and intrinsic motivating factors

Extrinsic rewards provided by the employer, including pay, will be important in attracting and retaining employees and, for limited periods, increasing effort and minimizing dissatisfaction. Intrinsic rewards related to responsibility, achievement and the work itself may have a longer-term and deeper impact on motivation.

The significance of needs and wants

People will be better motivated if their work experience satisfies their social and psychological needs as well as their economic needs.

The influence of goals

Individuals at work are motivated by having specific goals, and they perform better when they are aiming for difficult goals which they have accepted, and when they receive feedback on performance.

The importance of expectations

The degree to which people are motivated will depend not only upon the perceived value of the outcome of their actions – the goal or reward – but also upon their perceptions of the likelihood of obtaining a worthwhile reward, ie their expectations. They will be highly motivated if they can control the means to attain their goals.

The importance of job design

Job design is the process of deciding on the tasks that are involved in a role and how they should be carried out. There may be little room for variation in production line jobs but in others there is scope for non-financial motivation, especially by providing more autonomy as discussed in this chapter.

Approaches to motivation

Taking the lessons learnt from motivation theory into account, the approaches you can adopt to motivating people can be classified under three headings:

1 valuing people;
2 motivating them through financial rewards;
3 applying various forms of non-financial motivators.

Valuing people

Motivation will be enhanced if people feel that they are valued. This means investing in their success, trusting and empowering them, giving them the opportunity to be involved in matters with which they are concerned, keeping them fully in the picture, treating them fairly and like human beings, rather than 'resources' to be exploited in the interests of management, and recognizing the contribution they make.

Financial motivators

Money, in the form of pay or some other sort of remuneration, is the most obvious form of motivator. However, doubts have been cast on the effectiveness of money as a motivator by Herzberg because, he claimed, while the lack of it can cause dissatisfaction, its provision does not result in lasting satisfaction. There is something in this, especially for people on fixed salaries or rates of pay who do not benefit directly from an incentive scheme. They may feel good when they get an increase; apart from the extra money, it is a highly tangible form of recognition and an effective means of helping people to feel that they are valued. But this feeling of euphoria can rapidly die away. Other dissatisfactions from Herzberg's list of hygiene factors, such as working conditions or the quality of management, can loom larger in some people's minds when they fail to get the satisfaction they need from the work itself. However, it must be re-emphasized that different people have different needs and wants; some will be much more motivated by money than others. What cannot be assumed is that money motivates everyone in the same way and to the same extent. Thus it is naive to think that the introduction of a performance-related scheme will miraculously transform everyone overnight into well-motivated, high-performing individuals.

Nevertheless, money provides the means to achieve a number of different ends. It is a powerful force because it is linked directly or indirectly to the satisfaction of many needs. It clearly satisfies basic needs for survival and security, if it is coming in regularly. It can also satisfy the need for self-esteem (it is a visible mark of appreciation) and status – money can set you in a grade apart from your fellows and can buy you things they can't to build up your prestige. Money satisfies the less desirable but still prevalent drives of acquisitiveness and cupidity.

Money may in itself have no intrinsic meaning, but it acquires significant motivating power because it comes to symbolize so many intangible goals. It acts as a symbol in different ways for different people, and for the same person at different times. And pay is often the dominant factor in the choice of employer and pay considerations are powerful in binding people to their present job.

But do financial incentives motivate people? The answer is yes, for those people who are strongly motivated by money and whose expectations that they will receive a worthwhile financial reward are high. Money can motivate not only because people need and want it but also because it serves as a highly tangible means of recognition. However, less confident employees may not respond to incentives, which they do not expect to achieve. It is also argued that extrinsic rewards may erode intrinsic interest – people who work just for money could find their tasks less pleasurable and may not, therefore, do them so well. What we do know is that a multiplicity of factors is involved in performance improvements and only one of these is money.

But badly designed and managed pay systems can demotivate. Another researcher in this area was Eliot Jaques, who emphasized the need for such systems to be perceived as being fair and equitable (Jaques, 1961). In other words, the reward should be clearly related to effort or level of responsibility and people should not receive less money than they deserve compared with their fellow workers. Jaques called this the 'felt-fair' principle.

Non-financial motivators

From your point of view as a people manager money is not only an unreliable motivator but its provision as an incentive is often outside your control. Many public sector organizations and charities in the UK have pay spines in which pay progression is dependent on service rather than performance and line managers have little or no impact on the rate at which they progress. Even when pay is related to performance, line managers have to live with the system adopted by the organization. Their influence is often limited to rating people's performance but the amount distributed – which is usually too small to act as an incentive – is controlled by the management. Line managers have more control over non-financial rewards, including the intrinsic rewards, which, as noted above, can have a long-lasting effect on motivation. The main non-financial motivators are recognition, achievement, responsibility and autonomy, and opportunities for personal development and growth.

RECOGNITION

Recognition is one of the most effective methods of motivating people. They need to know not only how well they have achieved their objectives or carried out their work but also that their achievements are appreciated.

Recognition can be provided by positive and immediate feedback from you, which acknowledges what has been achieved. Simply saying thank you and explaining why you are pleased may be enough. You also recognize people when you listen to and act upon their suggestions. Other actions that provide recognition include allocation to a high-profile project, enlargement of the job to provide scope for more interesting and rewarding work, and recommending promotion.

Public 'applause' – letting everyone know that someone has done well – is another form of recognition. But it must be used with care. One person's recognition implies an element of non-recognition to others, and the consequences of having winners and losers need to be carefully managed.

Many organizations have formal recognition schemes which give managers scope, including a budget to provide individuals (and importantly, through them, their partners), with tangible means of recognition in the forms of gifts, vouchers, holidays or trips in the UK or abroad, days or weekends at health spas, or meals out. Team awards may be through outings, parties and meals. Managers can provide individuals and teams with small recognition rewards from their budget and can nominate people for larger awards.

The principles you need to bear in mind in providing recognition are that it:

- should be given for specially valued behaviours and exceptional effort as well as for special achievements;
- is about valuing people; it should be personalized so that people appreciate that it applies to them;
- needs to be applied equitably, fairly and consistently throughout your team;
- must be genuine, not used as a mechanistic motivating device;
- needs to be given as soon as possible after the achievement;
- should be available to all;
- should be available for teams as well as individuals to reward collective effort and avoid creating isolated winners.

ACHIEVEMENT

People feel rewarded and motivated if they are given the scope to achieve as well as being recognized for the achievement. University researchers, for example, want to enhance their reputation as well as making a significant contribution to their institution's research rating.

If achievement motivation is high it will result in discretionary behaviour. Discretionary or self-motivated behaviour occurs when people take control of situations or relationships, direct the course of events, create and seize opportunities, enjoy challenge, react swiftly and positively to new circumstances and relationships, and generally 'make things happen'. People who are driven by the need to achieve are likely to be proactive, to seek opportunities and to insist on recognition. You can develop achievement motivation by ensuring people know what they are expected to achieve, giving them the opportunity to achieve, providing the support and guidance that will enable them to achieve, and recognizing their achievements.

RESPONSIBILITY AND AUTONOMY

You can motivate people by giving them more responsibility for their own work and more autonomy in the sense that they can make their own decisions without reference to you. This is in line with the concept of intrinsic motivation. The scope for designing or redesigning roles varies according to the nature of the work. But where there is an opportunity it is worth seizing and methods of doing so are examined in Chapter 9.

OPPORTUNITY TO DEVELOP

Most people want to develop – to get a better or more interesting job and to advance their careers either through promotion or laterally by expanding their role. You can use this need as a motivator by providing learning and development opportunities, making use of what is available in the organization but also giving people additional responsibilities so that they gain experience with whatever support and guidance you need to give them.

TEN STEPS TO ACHIEVING HIGHER MOTIVATION

1 Agree demanding but achievable goals.

2 Create expectations that certain behaviours and outputs will produce worthwhile rewards when people succeed.

3 Provide feedback on performance.

4 Design jobs that enable people to feel a sense of accomplishment, to express and use their abilities, and to exercise their own decision-making powers.

5 Make good use of the organization's reward system to provide appropriate financial incentives.

6 Provide recognition and praise for work well done.

7 Communicate to your team and its members the link between performance and reward, thus enhancing expectations.

8 Provide effective leadership.

9 Give people guidance and training that will develop the knowledge and skills they need to improve their performance and be rewarded accordingly.

10 Offer opportunities for learning and development, which will enable them to advance their careers.

EXERCISE 4.1

What do you know about motivation?

Test your knowledge of motivation by selecting what you think is the best answer for each of the following multiple-choice questions. There may be some merit in each of the alternatives but you should choose the one which, on balance, you prefer.

1 Motivation is:

(a) the goals individuals have;

(b) the ways in which individuals choose their goals;

(c) the ways in which others try to change their behaviour;

(d) the strength and direction of behaviour.

2 Intrinsic motivation:

(a) is motivation which arises from the work itself;

(b) is caused by internal factors such as personality;

(c) is always to be preferred to extrinsic motivation;

(d) results from policies which recognize achievement.

3 Extrinsic motivation:

(a) has an immediate, powerful and long-lasting effect on performance;

(b) takes place when things are done to or for people to motivate them;

(c) is provided by performance-related pay;

(d) is generated by effective leadership.

4 Which step in the motivational process follows after identification of a need and a means of satisfying a need?

(a) performance;

(b) goal-directed behaviour;

(c) rewards or punishments;

(d) reassessment of needs.

5 The key message of goal theory is that:

(a) people are only motivated when they agree their goals;

(b) people will only be motivated if they are set challenging goals;

(c) the achievement of goals provides a highly effective form of motivation;

(d) feedback on performance in the best way to motivate people.

6 Expectancy theory:

(a) states that people are motivated when they expect that their behaviour will produce a worthwhile reward;

(b) provides a useful basis for assessing the effectiveness of a performance pay scheme;

(c) states that people expect to be rewarded financially in accordance with their contribution;

(d) states that people's expectations determine the extent to which they are motivated.

7 Money is:

(a) the most effective method of motivation;

(b) more effective as a motivator with some people than others;

(c) an unsatisfactory method of motivation because its impact does not last long;

(d) only effective as a motivator if is distributed fairly.

8 The best way to motivate people is to:

(a) design jobs which are intrinsically satisfying;

(b) reward good performance and punish poor performance;

(c) rely on an appropriate combination of financial and non-financial motivators;

(d) set people demanding ('stretch') goals.

SUMMARY POINTS

- Motivation is the process of getting people to move in the direction you want them to go.

- A motive is a reason for doing something. Motivation is concerned with the factors that influence people to behave in certain ways.

- Motivation is initiated by the recognition of an unsatisfied need. A goal is then established which it is believed will satisfy this need and a decision is made on the action, which it is expected will achieve the goal.

- The two types of motivation are intrinsic motivation and extrinsic motivation.

- People are motivated when they feel valued. This can be achieved by both financial and non-financial means.

5 Enhancing engagement

The term 'engagement' has come to the fore fairly recently. It is sometimes used very loosely as a powerful notion which embraces pretty well everything the organization is seeking with regard to the contribution and behaviour of its employees in terms of levels of job performance, willingness to do more and identification with the organization. More precisely, employee engagement is defined as what takes place when people at work are interested in and positive, even excited about their jobs. They are prepared to go the extra mile to get their work done to the best of their ability by exercising 'discretionary effort', ie doing more than is normally expected of them – things that are not in their job description.

Drivers of engagement

Engagement is best enhanced when employees have meaningful work that effectively uses their skills and provides them with freedom to exercise choice. Engaged employees feel that their jobs are an important part of who they are. Employees are also more likely to be engaged when they are supported, recognized, and developed by their managers and when they have a say in matters that affect them. Lands' End, the clothing mail order company, believes that staff who are enjoying themselves, who are being supported and developed and who feel fulfilled and respected at work, will provide the best service to customers.

CASE STUDY: TELEFÓNICA O2 UK

Extract from Engaging for Success: Enhancing performance through employee engagement *(MacLeod and Clarke, 2009), reproduced under Crown Copyright.*

The seven-point People Promise outlines O2's commitment to creating the best possible employee experience.

- It promises its people a warm welcome, providing a full induction programme and welcome day for all new starters.
- People are given the opportunity to get on. Everyone forms a personal development plan with their manager and talks through their career goals at least twice a year. People can learn new skills by applying for a matched contribution Learning Scheme or by using the online academies which offer training on a broad range of subjects.
- O2 wants to create a workplace where people trust their senior managers and their line manager. It invests heavily in the leadership skills of its managers, affirming your manager will be there for you.
- O2 people are trusted to do a great job. They're encouraged to suggest new ways of doing things in advisor forums, manager forums, skip-level meetings and Ignite, an online system enabling advisors to capture customer insights and share their own.
- O2 wants to be a great place to work. In the current economic climate, it is focusing even harder on looking after

its people, improving its total reward offering by introducing new flexible benefits and a broad range of discounts with high street retailers. Vielife, an online health and well-being programme, helps people manage their sleep, nutrition, stress and physical activity. And O2 Confidential offers free 24-hour advice on issues including benefits, debt, housing, and other financial matters.

- O2 people should feel part of something special. For example, people are encouraged to volunteer for charities and may be afforded time out for their chosen projects. And they can apply for awards or refer friends and family under the It's Your Community programme, which gives grants of up to £1,000 to community projects all over the UK.

- O2 says thanks for a job well done, praising its people and giving them recognition for their work. A new scheme launching this year will highlight outstanding individual and team contributions to strategic goals, offering people high street vouchers and the chance to attend a glittering annual ceremony.

What managers can do

Managers play a vital and immediate part in increasing levels of employee engagement. They do this by exercising leadership and ensuring that their team members are clear about what they have to do, acquire the skills required and appreciate the significance of their contribution. They have considerable influence over job and work design and are there to provide support, encouragement and coaching with the help of the performance management system.

TEN STEPS TO ENHANCING ENGAGEMENT

1 Delegate more.

2 Involve people in setting their targets and standards of performance and in deciding on performance measures.

3 Allow individuals and teams more scope to plan, act and monitor their own performance.

4 Involve people in developing their own solutions to problems.

5 Create self-managed teams – ones that set their own objectives and standards and manage their own performance.

6 Give people a voice in deciding what needs to be done.

7 Help people to learn from their own mistakes.

8 Encourage continuous development so that people can both grow in their roles and grow their roles.

9 Share your vision and plans with members of your team.

10 Trust people and treat them as adults.

EXERCISE 5.1

Dealing with engagement problems

You are the head of a major division of your large financial services company. Your division has six departments, each controlled by a senior manager, and there are 46 middle managers and team leaders. There are 380 professional, administrative and support staff working in the division.

There have been a number of problems with high staff turnover and absenteeism in your division, and productivity has declined. In discussions first with the HR director and then with top management it has been agreed that this appears to be a case of low levels of engagement. The HR director therefore organized an engagement survey with the results shown below. Eighty-three staff completed the survey (a high response rate, showing their concern) and the percentages expressing different levels of opinion about the 10 statements are shown in the appropriate boxes on the form.

You are now asked to comment on the results and make suggestions to the management board about what needs to be done.

ENGAGEMENT SURVEY

Please indicate your department and section in the spaces below. This survey is anonymous so you do not need to give your name.

Department..**Section**..

Please place a tick in the box which most closely fits your opinion

OPINION	STRONGLY AGREE	INCLINED TO AGREE	NEITHER AGREE NOR DISAGREE	INCLINED TO DISAGREE	STRONGLY DISAGREE
1 I am very satisfied with the work I do	5%	15%	18%	40%	22%
2 My job is interesting	6%	12%	26%	34%	10%
3 I know exactly what I am expected to do	9%	16%	32%	39%	4%
4 I am prepared to put myself out to do my work	6%	14%	28%	40%	12%
5 My job is not very challenging	43%	31%	12%	10%	4%
6 I am given plenty of freedom to decide how to do my work	4%	17%	24%	31%	24%
7 I get plenty of opportunities to learn in this job	2%	4%	12%	52%	30%
8 The facilities/equipment/ tools provided are excellent	15%	27%	45%	11%	2%
9 I do not get adequate support from my boss	12%	31%	34%	17%	6%
10 I like working for my boss	9%	12%	29%	31%	9%

SUMMARY POINTS

- Engagement is defined as what takes place when people at work are interested in and positive, even excited about their jobs.

- Engagement is best enhanced when employees have meaningful work that effectively uses their skills and provides them with freedom to exercise choice – engaged employees feel that their jobs are an important part of who they are.

- Managers play a vital and immediate part in increasing levels of employee engagement. They do this by exercising leadership and ensuring that their team members are clear about what they have to do, acquire the skills required and appreciate the significance of their contribution.

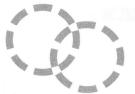

6 Organizing people

The management of people in organizations constantly raises questions such as 'Who does what?', 'How should activities be grouped together?', 'What lines and means of communication need to be established?' and 'Are we doing everything that we ought to be doing and nothing that we ought not to be doing?'

As a manager or team leader you might have been promoted, transferred or recruited into your post and been presented with an established organization structure – a framework for getting things done. Very occasionally, you may have to set up your own organization. More frequently, you may feel that there are improvements that can usefully be made to the structure or to the ways in which responsibilities and tasks are allocated to members of your team. To do this it is necessary to understand the process and aim of organizing and the guidelines for organizing, as explained in this chapter.

The process of organizing

The formal process of organizing can be described as the design, development and maintenance of a system of coordinated activities in which individuals and groups of people work cooperatively under leadership towards commonly understood and accepted goals. This may involve the grand design or redesign of the total structure, but most frequently it is concerned with the organization of particular functions and activities and the basis upon which the relationships between them are managed.

There are four important points to bear in mind about organizations:

1 Formal organization structures are based on laid-down hierarchies (lines of command), which are represented in organization charts. Typically, use is made of closely defined job descriptions. But to varying extents they function informally as well as formally by means of a network of roles and relationships which cut across formal organizational boundaries and lines of command.

2 Organizations are not static things. Changes are constantly taking place in the business itself, in the environment in which the business operates, and in the people who work in the business.

3 Organizations consist of people working more or less cooperatively together. Inevitably, and especially at managerial levels, the organization may have to be adjusted to fit the particular strengths and attributes of the people available. The result may not conform to the ideal, but it is more likely to work than a structure which ignores the human element. It is always desirable to have an ideal structure in mind, but it is equally desirable to modify it to meet particular circumstances, as long as there is awareness of the potential problems that may arise. This may seem an obvious point, but it is frequently ignored by management consultants and others who adopt a doctrinaire approach to organization, sometimes with disastrous results.

4 The form of organization will depend on its purpose, activities and context. Thus a highly structured form of 'line and staff' or 'command and control' organization would be right in a bureaucracy or any business where the work is regulated and predictable. A different structure might be needed in an organization such as a management consultancy which operates as a matrix with a number of disciplines from which individuals are selected to operate in temporary groups.

Aim

Bearing in mind the need to take an empirical approach, the aim of organizing in a typical business or business unit could be defined as being to optimize the arrangements for conducting its affairs. To do this it is necessary, as far as circumstances require and allow, to:

- clarify the overall purposes of the organization or organizational unit;
- define the key activities required to achieve that purpose;
- group these activities logically together to avoid unnecessary overlap or duplication;
- ensure that the system of work provides for a logical flow of activities without duplication;
- be careful about the use of 'pipe lines' – splitting up an overall activity into a number of sub-units through each of which the work is supposed to flow; although seemingly efficient, such an arrangement can result in duplication, delays and the creation of jobs which may be demotivating because of their routine nature and limited scope for discretion;
- avoid the creation of 'silos', ie departments or sections which focus too much on their own activities and take no account of what other related organizational units do;
- provide for the integration of activities and the achievement of cooperative effort and teamwork in pursuit of the common purpose;
- build flexibility into the system so that organizational arrangements can adapt quickly to new situations and challenges;
- clarify individual roles, accountabilities and authorities;
- design jobs to make the best use of the skills and capacities of the job holders and to provide them with high levels of intrinsic motivation.

Organizational guidelines

No absolute standards exist against which an organization structure can be judged. There is no such thing as an ideal organization; there is never one right way of organizing anything and there are no invariable principles governing organizational choice. But there are some guidelines as described below that you can refer to if faced with the job of setting up or reviewing an organization. They are not absolutes but they are worth considering in the light of your analysis of the needs of the situation:

- Allocation of work – the work that has to be done should be defined and allocated to work teams, project groups and individual positions. Related activities should be grouped together.

- Differentiation and integration – it is necessary to differentiate between the different activities that have to be carried out, but it is equally necessary to ensure that these activities are integrated so that everyone in the team is working towards the same goals.

- Teamwork – jobs should be defined and roles described in ways which facilitate and underline the importance of teamwork. Areas where cooperation is required should be emphasized. Wherever possible, self-managing teams should be set up with the maximum amount of responsibility to run their own affairs, including planning, budgeting and exercising quality control. Networking should be encouraged in the sense of people communicating openly and informally with one another as the need arises. It should be recognized that these informal processes can be more productive than rigidly 'working through channels' as set out in an organization chart.

- Flexibility – the structure should be flexible enough to respond quickly to change, challenge and uncertainty. At management levels a 'collegiate' approach to team operation should be considered in which people share responsibility and are expected to work with their colleagues in areas outside their primary function or skill.

- Role clarification – people should be clear about their roles as individuals and as members of a team. They should know what they will be held accountable for and be given every opportunity to use their abilities in achieving objectives which they have agreed and are committed to. Role profiles should define key result areas but should not act as straitjackets, restricting initiative and unduly limiting responsibility. Elaborate job descriptions listing every task are unnecessary as they limit flexibility and authority and, because they appear to be comprehensive, invite some people to make the remark that 'It is not in my job description'.

- Decentralization – authority to make decisions should be delegated as close to the scene of action as possible.

- De-layering – too many layers create unnecessary 'pecking orders', inhibit communications and limit flexibility.

- Span of control – there is a limit to the number of people one manager or team leader can control although this limit varies according to the nature of the work and the people who carry it out. In fact, you can work with a far larger span than you imagine as long as you are prepared to delegate more, avoid becoming involved in too much detail and concentrate on developing good teamwork.

- 'One-over-one' relationships – situations in which a single manager controls another single manager who in turn controls a team of people can cause confusion as to who is in charge and how the duties of the two people in the one-over-one relationship are divided.

- One person one boss – ideally individuals should be responsible to one person so they know where they stand. One of the main exceptions to this rule occurs when someone has a direct 'line' responsibility to a manager but also has a 'functional' responsibility to a senior member of the individual's function, who is concerned with maintaining corporate standards for the function and dealing with corporate policies. But in such cases the way in which functional responsibility is exercised and its limits have to be defined and, usually, it is understood that individuals are accountable to their line manager for achieving results within their department or team.

EXERCISE 6.1

Case study: Work and organization design in Barchester Council
Barchester Council has launched a major initiative called 'The change project'. This is an organization-wide programme, the aim of which was to establish how the council, while under intensive pressure to reduce expenditure, could continue to provide high-quality and joined-up services and still cut costs.

The starting point for the initiative was the Housing Department, which was known to be functioning poorly. An investigation by the HR department revealed serious deficiencies in the ways in which the council delivered services to its customers. People visiting the department for the first time would find themselves being passed between a number of different people in different sections of the department, each with certain responsibilities involved in housing. So, for example, customers might have to see a housing adviser, a homeless persons officer, a registrations officer, an allocations officer, then perhaps a temporary accommodation officer, then maybe an income officer – all of which was overseen and checked by a manager. A customer could come in at 9:00 and might not leave until 17:30, having been passed around all these different people.

The service was complicated, time consuming and frustrating for those using it, while at the same time involving a great deal of resources, which was not always efficient nor effective. There were delays and wastes, often because of the historical way services had developed. Each section worked within strictly defined limits – no flexibility was allowed. Staff often had limited knowledge of how other teams worked and 'silo' working was typically the norm.

The jobs in the sections were reduced to a number of strictly defined tasks and individual administrators had little or no discretion to make decisions. The staff were generally bored and frustrated because they were limited to carrying out highly routine work with no variety. This resulted in poor morale, which undoubtedly affected the level of service to customers.

On the basis of this information, what could be done to improve the service?

SUMMARY POINTS

- The formal process of organizing can be described as the design, development and maintenance of a system of coordinated activities in which individuals and groups of people work cooperatively under leadership towards commonly understood and accepted goals.

- The aim of organizing in a typical business or business unit could be defined as being to optimize the arrangements for conducting its affairs. Organizations function informally as well as formally.

- Organizations are not static things. Changes are constantly taking place.

- It is always desirable to have an ideal structure in mind, but it is equally desirable to modify it to meet particular circumstances.
- The form of organization will depend on its purpose, activities and context.
- No absolute standards exist against which an organization structure can be judged.

There is no such thing as an ideal organization; there is never one right way of organizing anything and there are no absolute principles governing organizational choice. But there are some guidelines, as described in this chapter.

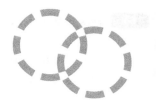

7 Team building

One of your most important roles as a manager is to act as a team builder – developing and making the best use of the capacity of your team so that its members jointly deliver superior levels of performance.

Team building takes place when you clarify the team's purpose and goals, ensure that its members work well together, strengthen the team's collective skills, enhance commitment and confidence, remove externally imposed obstacles and create opportunities for team members to develop their skills and competencies.

To undertake this task you need to get answers to these questions:

- What is a team?
- What are the factors that contribute to team effectiveness?
- How should team performance be assessed?
- How should team performance reviews be conducted?
- Overall, what needs to be done to obtain good teamwork?

What is a team?

A team is a group of people with complementary skills who work together to achieve a common purpose. The team leader sets the direction, provides guidance and support, coordinates the team's activities, ensures that each team member plays his or her part, promotes the learning and development of team members, consults with the team on issues affecting its work and, in conjunction with team members, monitors and reviews team performance.

However, some organizations have developed the concept of self-managing teams which are largely autonomous. They are responsible to a considerable degree for planning and scheduling work, problem solving, developing their own key performance indicators and setting and monitoring team performance and quality standards. The role of their team leaders is primarily to act as coordinators and facilitators; their style is expected to be more supportive and facilitative than directive.

What are the factors that contribute to team effectiveness?

An effective team is likely to be one whose purpose is clear and whose members feel the task is important, both to them and the organization. The structure and methods of operation are relevant to the requirements of the task. Team members will be highly engaged in the work they do together and committed to the team's overall group task. They will have been grouped together in a way that means that they are related to one another through the requirements of task performance and task interdependence. The team will use discretionary effort – going the extra mile – to achieve its task. There will be effective leadership setting the direction and providing guidance without dominating the group. The main features of well-functioning teams are that:

- the atmosphere tends to be informal, comfortable and relaxed;
- team members listen to each other and work well together;
- team members are multi-skilled as required to get the task done;
- many decisions are reached by consensus;
- action is taken by means of assignments that are clear and accepted;
- team leaders provide effective leadership but do not dominate their teams – the issue is not who controls but how to get the work done.

How should team performance be assessed?

The performance of teams should be assessed in terms of their output and results and the quality of team processes that have contributed to those results.

Output criteria include the achievement of team goals, customer satisfaction and the quantity and quality of work. Process measures comprise participation, collaboration and collective effort, conflict resolution, joint decision making, planning and goal setting, interpersonal relations, interdependence, and adaptability and flexibility.

How should team performance reviews be conducted?

Good support to your team-building efforts will be provided if you conduct regular team performance review meetings to assess feedback and control information on their joint achievements against objectives and to discuss any issues concerning teamwork. The agenda for such meetings could be as follows:

1 General feedback review of the progress of the team as a whole, problems encountered by the team that have caused difficulties or hampered progress, and helps and hindrances to the operation of the team.

2 Work reviews of how well the team has functioned.

3 Group problem solving including an analysis of reasons for any shortfalls or other problems, and agreement of what needs to be done to solve them and prevent their re-occurrence.

4 Update objectives – review of new requirements, opportunities or threats and the amendment of objectives as required.

Use can be made of the following 10-point checklist.

TEAM PERFORMANCE CHECKLIST

1 How effective are we at achieving team goals?

2 How well do we work together?

3 Does everyone contribute?

4 How effectively is the team led?

5 How good are we at analysing problems and making decisions?

6 How good are we at initiating action?

7 Do we concentrate sufficiently on the priority issues?

8 Do we waste time on irrelevancies?

9 To what extent can team members speak their minds without being squashed by others?

10 If there is any conflict, is it openly expressed and is it about issues rather than personalities?

What needs to be done to achieve good teamwork?

TEN THINGS TO DO WHEN BUILDING YOUR TEAM

1 Establish urgency and direction.

2 Select members based on skills and skill potential, who are good at working with others but still capable of taking their own line when necessary.

3 Pay particular attention to first meetings and actions.

4 Agree with team members immediate performance-orientated tasks and goals, including overlapping or interlocking objectives for people who work together. These will take the

form of targets to be achieved or tasks to be accomplished by joint action.

5 Assess people's performance not only on the results they achieve but also on the degree to which they are good team members. Recognize people who have been good team workers.

6 Recognize good team performance by praise and rewards for the team as a whole.

7 Build team spirit with out-of-work activities.

8 Hold team meetings to review performance, focusing on team process as well as outputs.

9 Provide learning and development opportunities so that team members can become multi-skilled or at least improve the level of their existing skills.

10 Make use of any learning activities provided by the organization that focus on teamwork.

EXERCISE 7.1

Investigating the quality of teamwork

You are the manager of a large department in a mail order company. There are six work teams in the department with an average of eight people in each team. Productivity in the department has fallen recently and you think an important contributory factor is the quality of teamwork. You have noticed a number of instances where teams do not seem to be working effectively. You therefore asked your HR director to investigate. She conducted a survey of the 48 team members, 40 of whom responded. The results are shown below. What do these indicate and what needs to be done?

TEAM EFFECTIVENESS SURVEY

Please indicate your department and section in the spaces below. This survey is anonymous so you do not need to give your name.

Department..**Section**...

Please place a tick in the box which most closely fits your opinion

OPINION	STRONGLY AGREE	INCLINED TO AGREE	NEITHER AGREE NOR DISAGREE	INCLINED TO DISAGREE	STRONGLY DISAGREE
1 The team's goals are clear and understood	3	6	8	15	8
2 The team members work well together	8	10	16	4	2
3 The team is able to withstand pressure	6	9	18	5	2
4 The team gets on well with other teams	4	6	12	15	3
5 The team is able to manage itself in terms of allocating work, setting priorities and monitoring performance	2	5	21	8	4
6 The quality of leadership exercised by the team leader is high	0	1	8	20	11
7 The level and range of skills possessed by individual team members is high	10	16	10	4	0
8 Team members work flexibly, taking advantage of their multi-skilling capabilities	1	11	21	13	2

SUMMARY POINTS

- Team building takes place when you clarify the team's purpose and goals, ensure that its members work well together, strengthen the team's collective skills, enhance commitment and confidence, remove externally imposed obstacles and create opportunities for team members to develop their skills and competencies.

- A team is a group of people with complementary skills who work together to achieve a common purpose.

- The team leader sets the direction, provides guidance and support, coordinates the team's activities, ensures that each team member plays his or her part, promotes the learning and development of team members, consults with the team on issues affecting its work and, in conjunction with team members, monitors and reviews team performance.

- In an effective team its purpose is clear and its members feel the task is important. The structure and methods of operation are appropriate relevant to the requirements of the task and team members will be highly engaged in the work they do together. There will be effective leadership which sets the direction and provides guidance without dominating the group.

8 Delegating

You can't do everything yourself, so you have to delegate – get other people to do some or all of the work. It is one of the most important things you do. At first sight delegation looks simple; just tell people what you want them to do and then let them get on with it. But there is more to it than that. It is not easy. It requires courage, patience and skill. And it is an aspect of your work in which you have more freedom of choice than in any other of your activities. What you choose to delegate, to whom and how, is almost entirely at your discretion.

This chapter provides answers to the following questions about delegation:

- What is it?
- What are its advantages?
- What are the difficulties?
- When do you delegate?
- What do you delegate?
- How do you delegate?
- How can you assess whether you are good at delegating?

What is delegation?

Delegation is not the same as handing out work. There are some things that your team members do that go with the territory. They are part of their normal duties and all you have to do is to define what those duties are and allocate work accordingly.

Delegation is different. It takes place when you deliberately give someone the authority to carry out a piece of work you could have decided to keep and carry out yourself. Bear in mind that what you are doing is delegating authority to carry out a task and make the decisions this involves. You are still accountable for the results achieved. It is sometimes said that you cannot delegate responsibility but this is misleading if responsibility is defined, as it usually is, as what people are expected to do – their work, their tasks and their duties. What you cannot do is delegate accountability. In the last analysis you as the manager or team leader always carry the can. What managers have to do is to ensure that people have the authority to carry out their responsibilities. A traffic warden without the power to issue tickets would have to be exceedingly persuasive to have any chance of dealing with parking offences.

What are the advantages of delegation?

The advantages of delegation are that:

1 It enables you to focus on the things that really matter in your job – those aspects which require your personal experience, skill and knowledge.
2 It relieves you of less critical and routine tasks.
3 It frees you from being immersed in detail.
4 It extends your capacity to manage.
5 It reduces delay in decision making – as long as authority is delegated close to the scene of action.
6 It allows decisions to be taken at the level where the details are known.

7 It empowers and motivates your staff by extending their responsibilities and authority and providing them with greater autonomy.

8 It develops the knowledge and skills of your staff and increases their capacity to exercise judgement and make decisions.

What are the difficulties of delegation?

The advantages of delegation are compelling but there are difficulties. The main problem is that delegation often involves risk. You cannot be absolutely sure that the person to whom you have delegated something will carry out the work as you would wish. The temptation therefore is to over-supervise, breath down people's necks and interfere. This inhibits their authority, makes them nervous and resentful and destroys their confidence, thus dissipating any advantages the original act of delegation might have had. Many managers are reluctant to delegate because they want to keep on top of everything. They really think they know best and cannot trust anyone else to do it as well as them, never mind better. Some managers are reluctant to delegate simply because they enjoy what they are doing and cannot bear the possibility of giving it away to anyone else.

Approaches to delegation

To a degree, overcoming these difficulties is a matter of simply being aware of them and appreciating that if there any disadvantages, these are outweighed by the advantages. But approaches to delegation such as those discussed below help. You need to understand the process of delegation, when to delegate, what to delegate, how to choose people to whom you want to delegate, how to give out the work and how to monitor performance.

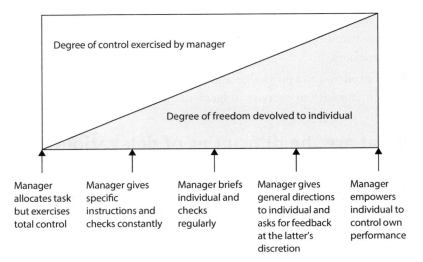

Degree of control exercised by manager

Degree of freedom devolved to individual

| Manager allocates task but exercises total control | Manager gives specific instructions and checks constantly | Manager briefs individual and checks regularly | Manager gives general directions to individual and asks for feedback at the latter's discretion | Manager empowers individual to control own performance |

FIGURE 8.1 The sequence of delegation

The process of delegation

Delegation is a process which starts from the point when total control is exercised (no freedom of action for the individual to whom work has been allocated) to full devolution (the individual is completely empowered to carry out the work). This sequence is illustrated in Figure 8.1.

When to delegate

You should delegate when you:

- have more work than you can carry out yourself;
- cannot give sufficient time to your priority tasks;
- want to develop a member of your team;
- believe that it will increase someone's engagement with their job;
- think that the job can be done adequately by the individual or the team to whom you delegate.

What to delegate

The tasks you delegate are ones that you don't need to do yourself. You are not just ridding yourself of the difficult, tedious or unrewarding tasks. Neither are you trying simply to win for yourself an easier life. In some ways delegation will make your life more difficult, but also more rewarding.

You delegate routine and repetitive tasks that you cannot reasonably be expected to do yourself – as long as you use the time you have won productively.

You can delegate specialist tasks to those who have the skills and know-how to do them. You cannot be expected to do it all yourself. Neither can you be expected to know it all yourself. You have to know how to select and use expertise. There will be no problem as long as you make it clear what you want from the experts and get them to present it to you in a useable way. As their manager you should know what your specialists can do for you and you should be knowledgeable enough about the subject to understand whether or not what they produce is worth having.

You delegate to a team when you ask people collectively to carry out a task which you previously did yourself and which you are confident they can do.

Choosing who does the work

When delegating to individuals the person you choose to do the work should ideally have the knowledge, skills, experience, motivation and time needed to get it done to your satisfaction. It is your job as a manager or team leader to know your people – their strengths and weakness, what they are good at or not so good at, those who are willing to learn and those who, without good cause, think that they know it all.

Frequently you will want to delegate work to an individual who has less than the ideal experience, knowledge or skills. In these cases you should try to select someone who has intelligence, natural aptitude and, above all, willingness to learn how to do the job with help and guidance. This is how people develop, and the development of your team members should be your conscious aim whenever you delegate.

You are looking for someone you can trust. You don't want to over-supervise, so you have to believe that the person you select will get on with it and have the sense to come to you when stuck or before making a bad mistake. Of course you have to make it clear that you are there to give support and guidance when necessary, especially when a person is starting on an unfamiliar task. Initially, you may have to spend time coaching the individual to develop new or improved skills.

How do you know whom you can trust? The best way is to try people out first on smaller and less important tasks and give them more scope when they demonstrate they can do them. You may start by supervising them fairly closely but you can progressively let go until they are finally working mainly on their own with only periodical checks on progress. If they get on well, their sense of responsibility and powers of judgement will increase and improve and they will acquire the additional skills and confidence to justify your trust in their capacity to take on more demanding and responsible tasks.

Giving out the work

When you delegate you should ensure that the individuals or team concerned understand:

- why the work needs to be done;
- what they are expected to do;
- the date by which they are expected to do it;
- the end results they are expected to achieve;
- the authority they have to make decisions;

- the problems they must refer back;
- the progress or completion reports they should submit;
- any guidance and support that will be available to them.

You have to consider how much guidance will be required on how the work should be done. You don't want to give directions in such laborious detail that you run the risk of stifling initiative. Neither do you want to infuriate people by explaining everything needlessly. As long as you are reasonably certain that they will do the job to your satisfaction without embarrassing you or seriously upsetting people, exceeding the budget or breaking the law, let them get on with it. Follow Robert Heller's golden rule: 'If you can't do something yourself, find someone who can and then let them get on with it in their own sweet way' (Heller, 1972).

You can make a distinction between hard and soft delegation. Hard delegation takes place when you tell someone exactly what to do and how to do it. You spell it out, confirm it in writing and make a note in your diary of the date when you expect the job to be completed. And then you follow up regularly.

Soft delegation takes place when you agree generally what has to be done and leave the individual to get on with it. You still agree limits of authority, define the outcomes you expect, indicate how you will review progress and lay down when exception reports should be made. An exception report is one that only deals with events out of the ordinary. It is based on the principle of management by exception, which means focusing on the key events and measures, which will show up good, bad or indifferent results – the exceptions to the norm – as a guide to taking action. This approach frees people to concentrate on the issues that matter.

You should always delegate by the results you expect. When you are dealing with an experienced and capable person you don't need to specify how the results should be achieved. In the case of less experienced people you have to exercise judgement on the amount of guidance required. Newcomers with little or no experience will need plenty of guidance. They are on a 'learning curve', ie they are gradually acquiring the knowledge and skills they need to reach the required level of performance. You are responsible for seeing that they progress steadily up the learning curve bearing in mind that everyone will be starting from a different point and learning at a different rate. It is during this period that you act as a coach or an instructor, helping people to learn and develop (see also Chapter 9). Even if you do not need to specify how the results should be achieved, it is a good idea when the delegation involves getting someone to solve a problem to ask them how they propose to solve it.

Monitoring performance

Delegation is not abdication. You are still accountable for the results obtained by the members of your team collectively and individually. The extent to which you need to monitor performance and how you do so depends on the individuals concerned and the nature of the task. If individuals or the team as a whole are inexperienced generally or are being specifically asked to undertake an unfamiliar task you may at first have to monitor performance carefully. But the sooner you can relax and watch progress informally the better. The ideal situation is when you are confident that the individual or team will deliver the results you want with the minimum of supervision. In such cases you may only ask for periodical exception reports.

For a specific task or project set target dates and keep a reminder of these in your diary so that you can check that they have been met. Don't allow people to become careless about meeting deadlines.

Without becoming oppressive, you should ensure that progress and exception reports are made when required so that you can agree any necessary corrective action. You should have indicated the extent to which people have the authority to act without reference to you. They must therefore expect to be criticized if they exceed their brief or fail to keep you informed. You don't want any surprises and your people must understand that keeping you in the dark is unacceptable.

Try to restrain yourself from interfering unnecessarily in the way the work is being done. After all, it is the results that count. Of course, you must step in if there is any danger of things going off the rails. Rash decisions, over-expenditure and ignoring defined and reasonable constraints must be prevented.

There is a delicate balance to be achieved between hedging people around with restrictions, which may appear petty, and allowing them license to do what they like. There are no absolute rules as to where this balance should be struck. Managing people is an art, not a science. But you should at least have some notion of what is appropriate based on your knowledge of the people concerned and the situation you are in. It's a judgement call but a judgement based on an understanding of the facts. The best delegators are those who have a comprehensive knowledge of the strengths and weaknesses of their team members and of the circumstances in which they work.

Above all, avoid 'river banking'. This happens when a boss gives a subordinate a task that is more or less impossible to do. As the subordinate is going down for the third time the boss can be observed in a remote and safe position on the river bank saying: 'It's easy really, all you need to do is to try a bit harder'.

EXERCISE 8.1

How good a delegator are you?

Check how good you are at delegating by selecting the appropriate response to the following statements. Use the outcome as a basis for taking any actions you think would reduce the problem and improve your approach to delegation.

DELEGATION CHECKLIST

BEHAVIOUR AS A DELEGATOR	FREQUENCY OF BEHAVIOUR			ANY ACTION REQUIRED
	OFTEN	OCCASIONALLY	NEVER	

1 Do you have to take work home at night?

2 Do you work longer hours than those you manage?

3 Are you frequently interrupted because people come to you with questions or for advice or decisions?

4 Do you spend part of your working time doing things for others, which they could do for themselves?

5 Do you feel that you have to keep a close watch on details if someone is to do a job right?

6 Do you get involved in details because you enjoy them although someone else could do them well enough?

7 Do you lack confidence in the abilities of your team members so that you are afraid to risk them taking on more responsibility?

8 Do you fail to ask your people for ideas about solving problems that arise in their work?

9 Do you avoid systematically analysing and assessing the abilities of your people in order to plan delegation?

10 Do you neglect to provide guidance and coaching to less experienced people so that you will be confident that you can delegate more to them?

SUMMARY POINTS

- Delegation takes place when you deliberately give someone the authority to carry out a piece of work that you could have decided to keep and carry out yourself.

- The main advantage of delegation is that it enables you to focus on the things that really matter in your job – those aspects which require your personal experience, skill and knowledge.

- The main problem with delegation is that it can involve risk. You cannot be absolutely sure that the person to whom you have delegated something will carry out the work as you would wish.

- The tasks you delegate are ones that you don't need to do yourself. You are not just ridding yourself of the difficult, tedious or unrewarding tasks. Neither are you trying simply to win for yourself an easier life. In some ways delegation will make your life more difficult, but also more rewarding.

- You should always delegate by the results you expect.

- When you delegate you should ensure that the individuals or team concerned understand why the work needs to be done, what they are expected to do, the authority they have to make decisions and the progress reports they should submit.

- Delegation is not abdication. You are still accountable for the results obtained by the members of your team, collectively and individually. You have to monitor performance but avoid breathing down people's necks.

9 Defining work

As a manager one of your most important tasks is to define the work the members of your team have to do. You may need to design or redesign jobs when new work comes your way or when changes take place to the system of work in your area of responsibility. You will have to ensure that your people understand the jobs they have to do, and although you can simply tell them what their job consists of it is better to define this in the form of a role profile. Additionally, on a day-to-day basis, you will be giving out work in the form of specific tasks you want someone to carry out.

Designing jobs

A system of work consists of what has to be done and how it is done in a particular area of activity. It may have been prescribed for you in, for example, a production line, and jobs in the system may have been standardized, for example customer liaison staff in a call centre. However, managers often have the scope to determine how work should be done and in these cases they need to know how to get the best results by designing jobs that maximize the engagement of job holders with their work. Fred Herzberg put it well when he said that if you want someone to do a good job give them a good job to do. As far as possible you should provide for:

- *interest* – a job which is interesting in itself, involves the completion of a whole and identifiable piece of work and contributes to a significant result;

- *challenge* – work which creates demanding goals for people;
- *variety* – the work involves a selection of skills and abilities;
- *autonomy* – the job holder has discretion to make decisions, exercise choice, schedule the work and decide on the procedures to carry it out, and is personally responsible for outcomes.

This process is known as job enrichment.

EXERCISE 9.1

A case of job enrichment

James Turner has just been appointed as Group HR Director for the Acme Publishing Group, which publishes a number of local newspapers and three trade journals. He is based in the group's headquarters in London where about 200 people are employed in marketing, finance and running the trade journals. There are specialized HR staff in each of the provincial newspapers but other than the Group HR Director there are no HR specialists in the headquarters office. The previous head of HR had been transferred from a middle-ranking job in one of the trade journals and concentrated on the more routine personnel jobs such as recruitment in headquarters, having little to do with the local newspapers. The remit for the new Group HR Director was to get to grips with a number of pressing issues although he still had to look after HR matters in headquarters. Top management had ruled out appointing an HR assistant on the grounds of expense.

He did, however, inherit a personal assistant, Jane Hardy. She was 23 and had been with the firm for two years. She had accepted a university place five years ago but the severe illness of her mother had prevented her taking it up. Instead, she took a secretarial course. Her previous boss had restricted her duties to typing, filing and looking after his engagement diary. She was underemployed and bored.

After he started, James Turner quickly appreciated that Jane was demotivated by her work and was capable of doing much more, as she was both intelligent and outgoing. He decided that this was a case in which job enrichment was appropriate.

What should James do?

TEN STEPS TO DESIGNING JOBS THAT ARE LIKELY TO ENHANCE ENGAGEMENT

1 Where possible, arrange for people to work on a complete activity or product, or a significant part of it which can be seen as a whole.

2 Combine interdependent tasks into a job.

3 Provide a variety of tasks within the job.

4 Arrange work in a way that allows individuals to influence their work methods and pace.

5 Include tasks that offer some degree of autonomy for employees in the sense of making their own decisions.

6 Ensure that individuals can receive feedback about how well they are doing, preferably by evaluating their performance themselves.

7 Provide employees with the information they need to monitor their performance and make decisions.

8 Provide internal and external customer feedback directly to employees.

9 As far as possible, ensure that the job is perceived by individuals as requiring them to use abilities they value in order to perform it effectively.

10 Provide opportunities for employees to achieve outcomes that they consider desirable, such as personal advancement in the form of increased pay, scope for developing expertise, improved status within a work group and a more challenging job.

Developing role profiles

As part of the process of organizing work you need to ensure that everyone is aware of what they have to achieve in each of the main aspects of their role – their key result areas. This will not only spell out their responsibilities but will also provide the basis for managing performance by agreeing goals and reviewing the results attained by reference to those goals. This can be set out in a basic role profile as shown below.

Role title: Database administrator.

Department: Information systems.

Purpose of role: To develop and support the operation of databases and their underlying environment.

Key result areas:

1 Identify database requirements for all projects that require data management in order to meet the needs of internal customers.

2 Develop project plans collaboratively with colleagues to deliver against their database needs.

3 Support underlying database infrastructure.

4 Liaise with system and software providers to obtain product information and support.

5 Manage project resources (people and equipment) within predefined budget and criteria, as agreed with line manager and originating department.

6 Allocate work to and supervise contractors on day-to-day basis.

7 Ensure security of the underlying database infrastructure through adherence to established protocols and develop additional security protocols where needed.

Basic role profiles provide the essential information needed by role holders to carry out their role and by managers to manage the performance of role holders. They are reasonably simple to prepare and this is the least you can do if you want to ensure that everyone understands what is expected of them.

But it can also be useful to note the knowledge and skills role holders require – what they need to know and be able to do to carry out their role. This helps to indicate where learning and development actions would be appropriate. In addition, the ways they are expected to carry out their role can be defined, ie behavioural expectations. Such descriptions are known as competencies and many organizations have what are called competency frameworks which indicate under a number of headings competency requirements for their employees. These can be referred to in role profiles, possibly with modifications to fit an individual role. An example of what such definitions look like for a data administrator's role is shown below.

Need to know:

- Database administration techniques.
- The features and application of the database software used by the business.

Need to be able to:

- Analyse and choose between options where the solution is not always obvious.
- Develop project plans and organize own workload on a timescale of 1–2 months.
- Adapt to rapidly changing needs and priorities without losing sight of overall plans and priorities.
- Interpret budgets in order to manage resources effectively within them.

- Negotiate with suppliers.
- Keep abreast of technical developments and trends, bring these into day-to-day work when feasible and build them into new project developments.

Behavioural competencies:

- Aim to get things done well and set and meet challenging goals.
- Analyse information from a range of sources and develop effective solutions/recommendations.
- Communicate clearly and persuasively, orally or in writing, dealing with technical issues in a non-technical manner.
- Work participatively on projects with technical and non-technical colleagues.
- Develop positive relationships with colleagues as the supplier of an internal service.

To develop a basic role profile it is necessary to agree with individual role holders the overall purpose of their role and its key result areas. The sort of questions you can ask to obtain this information include:

1 What is the overall purpose of your role?
2 What do you think are the most important things you have to do – your key result areas?
3 What do you believe you are expected to achieve in each of these areas?
4 How will you – or anyone else – know whether or not you have achieved them?

To extend a basic role profile to include knowledge and skills and competency requirements it is necessary to obtain answers to the following questions, ideally from the individual, although quite a lot of guidance may be required in some instances.

1 What does the role holder need to know to perform this role well?

2 What should the role holder be able to do to perform this role well?

3 What sort of behaviour is likely to lead to effective performance in each of the main areas of the role?

EXERCISE 9.2

Preparing a basic role profile

The following is an edited transcript of a role analysis meeting with a quality control technician in a food manufacturing company. Prepare a basic role profile on the basis of this information.

I am responsible to the product line manager for the quality control of the four products on our cooked meats product line. I have to check that they meet our quality standards. I do this by conducting regular tests of a sample of products. I also check the labelling and packaging from time to time to ensure that these are in line with the specifications. I have to know all about the specifications for each of the four products. This includes the basic ingredients, the mix of these ingredients, taste and smell, appearance and usability.

Our quality control guide lays down the standard tests and sample sizes. There is a range of tests including microbiological and chemical tests. Some are quite complex; others, such as visual tests of appearance, are relatively straightforward.

If there is a problem, I refer it initially to the product line manager so that she can deal with any issue over which she has control. I am expected to offer my opinion on what needs to be done if this is suggested by test results. If it is a more fundamental

---

problem concerning such things as ingredients, the mix or production methods the product line manager will refer them to product development. I have to explain my findings there.

I submit regular (monthly) reports which summarize the results of the tests and highlight any issues which in my view need to be addressed. I am not expected to make recommendations on how the issues should be resolved, although my opinion is sometimes sought by manufacturing and product development. I also attend regular quality control meetings where I am expected to report on any issues and join in discussions.

I will have done a good job if the tests and inspections I carry out are conducted thoroughly in accordance with the requirements of our quality control guide. I have to earn the respect of the product line manager as someone who knows what she is talking about. My reports need to be clear, readable and submitted on time. My opinions on quality must be evidence-based and I must be able to support my conclusions with that evidence. I know I have done a good job if I offer relevant and practical comments and suggestions to the product line manager, my boss and the product development department.

Giving out work

Giving out work means telling people to do something, or if you want to be less authoritarian (and treating people right is about that), asking them. You have to give orders sometimes but it is preferable to make a polite request when you can.

When you give out work you need to spell out what has to be done, why it has to be done (people will be better motivated if they know the reason for what they do), when the work has to be completed and how performance will be measured. It may also be necessary to explain how the work should be done if the person concerned is unfamiliar with the task. This means giving instructions in the following sequence:

1 Explain what has to be done.
2 Demonstrate the task.
3 Get the individual to practise the task.
4 Follow up to ensure that everything is going well.

This sequence is described in more detail in Chapter 12.

SUMMARY POINTS

Managers:

- have to define the work the members of their team do;
- need to know how to get the best results by designing jobs that maximize the engagement of job holders with their work by providing interest, challenge, variety and autonomy;
- need to ensure that everyone is aware of what they have to achieve in each of the main aspects of their role – their key result areas;
- achieve the above by preparing role profiles that provide the essential information needed by role holders to carry out their role and by managers to manage the performance of role holders;
- give out work, which means telling people to do something; or, if they want to be less authoritarian (and treating people right is about that), asking them.

10 Performance management

One of your most important, if not the most important of your responsibilities as a manager is to ensure that the members of your team achieve high levels of performance. You have to ensure that they understand what you expect from them, that you and they work together to review performance against those expectations, and that you jointly agree what needs to be done to improve performance and develop knowledge and skills. Many organizations have a formal performance management system to help managers fulfil these responsibilities but in the absence of such a system you will still be able to manage and improve the performance of your team if you carry out the performance management activities described in this chapter.

The process of performance management

Performance management takes place in the form of a continuous cycle as shown in Figure 10.1.

This is, in fact, the normal cycle of management. Performance management is a natural process – it is not an appraisal system imposed on line managers by the HR function. As a natural process of management, performance management involves:

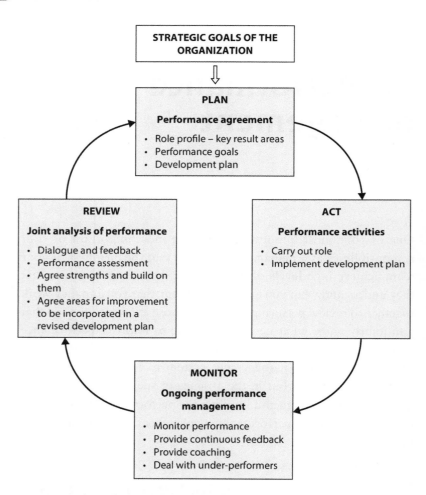

FIGURE 10.1 The performance management cycle

1 Planning – reaching agreement on objectives and standards to be achieved and the level of competence to be attained; discussing and agreeing development plans.

2 Action – taking action to implement plans and to achieve the required standards of day-to-day work. This action is carried out by individuals with the guidance and support of their managers.

3 Monitoring – actions and outcomes are monitored continuously by individuals and, as necessary, by their manager (the more this can be left to individuals so that they are in effect managing their own performance, the better).

4 Reviews – these can take place at any appropriate time during the year. Performance management is an all-the-year process, not an annual event. The reviews, also known as 'check-ins', can be quite informal with feedback from the manager or, preferably, generated by the individual from feedback information available directly to them. A more formal review should take place periodically, say once or twice a year.

Performance planning

Performance management is about getting people into action so that they achieve planned and agreed results. It focuses on what has to be done, how it should be done and what is to be achieved. But it is equally concerned with developing people – helping them to learn – and providing them with the support they need to do well, now and in the future. The framework for performance management is provided by the performance agreement, which is the outcome of performance planning. The agreement provides the basis for managing performance throughout the year and for guiding improvement and development activities. It is used as a reference point when reviewing performance and the achievement of development plans.

You should carry out performance planning jointly with the individual in order to reach agreement on what needs to be done.

The starting point is the role profile, which defines the results, knowledge and skills and behaviours required. This provides the basis for agreeing objectives and development plans as described below.

Agreeing objectives

Performance management is based on the definition of objectives for each key result area. Objective setting which results in an agreement on what the role holder has to achieve is an important part of the performance management processes of defining and managing expectations and forms the point of reference for performance reviews.

Objectives describe something that has to be accomplished. Objectives or goals (the terms are interchangeable) define what individuals are expected to achieve over a period of time.

Objectives can be agreed either as specific targets – eg 'reduce reject levels by 3 per cent within nine months', 'introduce x by y' – or as standards which indicate the conditions that will exist when a task has been well done – eg 'performance will be up to standard when reject rates are maintained below 2 per cent'.

The criteria for an effective performance objective in the form of a target or standard are that it should be:

- *aligned:* consistent with the goals and values of the organization and supporting their achievement;
- *relevant:* consistent with the purpose of the role;
- *precise:* specific, clear and well-defined – performance should be defined with a focus on valued outcomes such as quantity, quality, timeliness, cost effectiveness, need for supervision or impact on people;
- *measurable:* related to quantified or qualitative performance measures or standards;
- *trackable:* progress towards achieving the goal can be monitored;

- *challenging:* to stimulate high standards of performance and to encourage progress;
- *achievable:* performance goals should be achievable but not too easy – account should be taken of any constraints which might affect the individual's capacity to achieve the goals; these could include lack of resources (money, time, equipment, support from other people), lack of experience or training, and external factors beyond the individual's control;
- *agreed* by the manager and the individual concerned – the aim is to provide for the ownership, not the imposition, of goals, although there will be occasions where individuals have to be persuaded to accept a higher standard than they believe themselves to be capable of attaining and individual goals must be consistent with over-arching corporate goals;
- *time-related:* the timescale or date for reaching targets should be specified.

The acronym 'SMART' is often used to define a good performance objective. Traditionally, S stands for specific (sometimes stretching), M for measurable, A for agreed, R for realistic and T for time-related.

TEN-POINT CHECKLIST FOR SETTING OBJECTIVES

1 Has the objective-setting process been based on an agreed and up-to-date role profile which sets out key result areas?

2 Has objective setting been carried out jointly between the manager and the individual?

3 Are standards and targets clearly related to the key result areas in the role profile?

4 Do objectives support the achievement of team and corporate objectives?

5 Are the objectives specific?

6 Are they challenging?

7 Are they realistic and attainable?

8 Has a time limit for the achievement of targets been agreed?

9 How will the achievement of objectives be measured?

10 Have any problems in attaining these objectives been identified and has action to overcome these problems been agreed?

Development planning

Development plans spell out what employees, in conjunction as necessary with their managers, need to do in specified areas of their jobs such as reaching sales or productivity targets, working accurately, providing services to internal customers, cutting costs, reducing waste or meeting deadlines. In any development area, objectives should be set on what has to be done and by when, and agreement reached on how the expected results will be achieved. If there are any behavioural performance problems such as being uncooperative or lack of effort, plans are agreed on how the problems can be overcome. The plan should be focused; too many goals will only dissipate improvement efforts.

Development planning should also include the agreement of learning objectives, which, if achieved, will ensure that the employee meets the knowledge and skill requirements for effective performance in the role. These objectives can be set out in a personal development plan as described in Chapter 12.

Development plans take account of the outcome of the performance review held in the final stage of the performance management cycle. For those who have not been long enough in the job to have had a formal review, the development plan is based on a general assessment of the critical requirements for successful performance in each of the key result areas.

The continuing process of managing performance

You should treat your responsibility for managing performance as an integral part of the continuing process of management. This is based on a philosophy that emphasizes:

- the achievement of sustained improvements in performance;
- the continuous development of skills and capabilities;
- that the organization is a 'learning organization' in the sense that it is constantly developing and applying the learning gained from experience and the analysis of the factors that have produced high levels of performance.

You should therefore be ready, willing and able to monitor performance and define and meet development and improvement needs as they arise. As far as practicable, learning and work should be integrated. This means that encouragement should be given to your team members to learn from the successes, challenges and problems inherent in their day-to-day work.

You should carry out the process of monitoring performance by reference to agreed objectives and to agreed development plans. You may only need a light touch in monitoring performance if you are confident that an individual will deliver. In some cases you may have to monitor more closely. You have to decide how tightly you monitor on the basis of your understanding of the capacity of individuals to do the work. This is part of the delegation process as explained in Chapter 8.

An important part of the process of managing performance throughout the year is the provision of feedback as described below.

Providing feedback

Feedback is the provision of information to people on how they have performed in terms of results, events, critical incidents and significant behaviours. Feedback can be positive when it tells people that they have done well, constructive when it provides advice on how to do better, and negative when it tells people that they have done badly. Feedback reinforces effective behaviour and indicates where and how behaviour needs to change. It is provided by managers informally during the year or formally at a performance review meeting.

TEN GUIDELINES FOR PROVIDING FEEDBACK

1 *Build feedback into the job.* To be effective feedback should be built into the job or provided soon after the activity has taken place.

2 *Provide feedback on actual events.* Feedback should be given on actual results or observed behaviour. It should be backed up by evidence.

3 *Describe, don't judge.* The feedback should be presented as a description of what has happened; it should not be accompanied by a judgement.

4 *Refer to and define specific behaviours.* Relate all your feedback to specific items of behaviour. Don't indulge in transmitting general feelings or impressions.

5 *Emphasize the 'how' not the 'what'.* Focus attention more on how the task was tackled rather than on the result.

6 *Ask questions.* Ask questions rather than make statements – 'Why do you think this happened?'; 'On reflection is there any other way in which you think you could have handled the situation?'; 'How do you think you should tackle this sort of situation in the future?'

---

7 *Select key issues.* There is a limit to how much criticism anyone can take. If you overdo it, the shutters will go up and you will get nowhere. Select key issues and restrict yourself to them.

8 *Focus.* It is a waste of time to concentrate on areas that the individual can do little or nothing about. Focus on aspects of performance the individual can improve.

9 Provide *positive and constructive feedback.* People are more likely to work positively at improving their performance and developing their skills if they feel empowered by the process. Provide feedback on the things that the individual did well in addition to areas for improvement. Focus on what can be done to improve rather than on criticism.

10 *Ensure feedback leads to action.* Feedback should indicate any actions required to develop performance or skills.

Performance review meetings and check-ins

Formal performance review meetings are regarded by many organizations as a vital part of the process of managing performance. They are supposed to provide the opportunity to give feedback, to sound out from individuals how they feel about their job and provide the basis for development planning. But they are difficult to do well and can be stressful for the manager and the individual, both of whom may dread them. A number of companies have decided recently that annual reviews do more harm than good and have replaced them with more frequent and much less formal meetings, which are often called 'check-ins'.

Check-ins

A check-in takes the form of a guided conversation rather than a formal review. It includes feedback from the manager and, possibly, some self-assessment by the individual. Check-ins are rooted in the reality of what the individual is doing. They are concrete not abstract. They focus on strengths rather than dwelling on short-comings. Successes are recognized although things that have not gone according to plan will be noted in order to learn lessons for the future. Check-ins do not lead to a performance rating or the completion of a report, although a note can be taken of any agreed actions. They also provide opportunities for revising or renewing objectives and development plans.

However, in spite all the shortcomings of what has been called the dishonest annual ritual of a performance review, most com-panies with a performance management system insist on their managers conducting formal performance reviews once or some-times twice a year. If you work in that sort of company, guidelines on how to make the best of a bad job are set out below.

Formal performance reviews

Ideally, a review should take the form of a dialogue in which the two parties exchange comments and ideas and develop agreed plans. The conversation – and that is what it should be – should concentrate on analysis and review of the significant points emerg-ing from the period under consideration. It should be a joint affair – both parties are involved. So there may well be an element of self-assessment by the individual.

PREPARING FOR THE MEETING

The individual should be asked to prepare for the meeting by assessing the level of performance achieved and identifying any work issues.

As the manager, you should work your way through the follow-ing checklist of questions:

1 How well has the individual done in achieving agreed objectives during the review period?

2 How well have any improvement, development or training plans as agreed at the last review meeting been put into effect?

3 What should be the individual's objectives for the next review period?

4 Are you satisfied that you have given the individual sufficient guidance or help on what he/she is expected to do? If not, what extra help/guidance could you provide?

5 Is the best use being made of the individual's skills and abilities?

6 Is the individual ready to take on additional responsibilities?

7 Would the individual benefit from further experience?

8 Are there any special projects the individual could take part in which would help with his/her development?

9 What direction do you think the individual's career could take within the organization?

10 Does the individual need any further training?

CONDUCTING A PERFORMANCE REVIEW MEETING

To a degree, a performance review is a stocktaking process answering the questions 'where have we got to?' and 'how did we get here?' But there is much more to it than that. It is not just an historical exercise, dwelling on the past and taking the form of a post mortem. The true purpose of the review is to look forward to what needs to be done by people to achieve the overall purpose of their jobs, to meet new challenges, to make even better use of their skills, knowledge and abilities and to develop their skills and competencies to further their career and increase their employability.

A constructive review meeting is most likely to take place if you:

- encourage individuals to do most of the talking – the aim should be to conduct the meeting as a dialogue rather than using it to make 'top down' pronouncements on what you think about them;
- listen actively to what they say;

- allow scope for reflection and analysis;
- analyse performance not personality – concentrate on what individuals have done, not the sort of people they are;
- keep the whole period under review, not concentrating on isolated or recent events;
- adopt a 'no surprises' approach – performance problems should have been identified and dealt with at the time they occurred;
- recognize achievements and reinforce strengths;
- discuss any work problems, how they have arisen and what can be done about them;
- end the meeting positively with any necessary agreed action plans (learning and development and performance improvement).

DEALING WITH ISSUES

In a review meeting you have to deal with performance issues. Some will be positive, others may be negative. Dealing with negative points is often the area of greatest concern to line managers, many of whom do not like handing out criticisms. But this is not what performance reviews are about. They should not be regarded simply as an opportunity for attaching blame for something that has gone wrong in the past. If there has been a problem it should have been discussed when it happened. But this does not mean that persistent under-performance should go unnoticed during the review meeting. Specific problems may have been dealt with at the time but it may still be necessary to discuss a pattern of under-performance. The first step, and often the most difficult one, is to get people to agree that there is room for improvement. This will best be achieved if the discussion focuses on factual evidence of performance problems. Some people will never admit to being wrong and in those cases you may have to say in effect: 'Here is the evidence; I have no doubt that this is correct, and I am afraid you have to accept from me on the basis of this evidence that your performance in this respect has been unsatisfactory'.

EXERCISE 10.1

Conducting a performance review meeting
What should managers discuss with individuals at a review meeting?

SUMMARY POINTS

- One of the most important, if not the most important, responsibilities of a manager is to ensure that the members of their team achieve high levels of performance.

- Many organizations have a formal performance management system to help managers fulfil these responsibilities, but in the absence of such a system you will still be able to manage and improve the performance of your team if you carry out the performance management activities described in this chapter.

- Performance management takes place in the form of a continuous cycle as shown in Figure 10.1. It consists of four activities: planning, action, monitoring and reviews.

- The framework for performance management is provided by the performance agreement, which is the outcome of performance planning. The agreement includes objectives and a development plan.

- Objective setting, which results in an agreement on what the role holder has to achieve, is an important part of the performance management processes of defining and managing expectations and forms the point of reference for performance reviews.

- Objectives describe something that has to be accomplished. They can be agreed either as specific targets or as standards, which indicate the conditions that will exist when a task has been well done.

- Objectives should be aligned, relevant, precise, measurable, trackable, challenging, achievable, agreed and time-related.

- Development plans spell out what employees, in conjunction as necessary with their managers, need to do in specified areas of their jobs.

- The process of monitoring performance is carried out by reference to agreed objectives and to agreed development plans.

- An important part of the process of managing performance throughout the year is the provision of feedback.

- Formal performance review meetings are regarded by many organizations as a vital part of the process of managing performance. They are supposed to provide the opportunity to give feedback, to sound out from individuals how they feel about their job and provide the basis for development planning. But they are difficult to do well and can be stressful for the manager and the individual, both of whom may dread them. A number of companies have decided recently that annual reviews do more harm than good and have replaced them with more frequent and much less formal meetings, which are often called 'check-ins'.

- The following are the most important points to consider when conducting a performance review:

  - encourage individuals to do most of the talking;

  - recognize achievements and reinforce strengths;

  - analyse performance, not personality;

  - listen actively to what the individual says;

  - end the meeting positively with an agreed development plan.

11 Selection interviewing

As a manager, one of your most important people management tasks will be to interview candidates for a position on your team. Even when an HR (human resources) department or a recruitment agency is involved the final decision is yours or at least shared between you and your boss. The problem is that many managers think that they are good at selecting people but aren't. This is often revealed by an analysis of leavers which shows that a large proportion leave in the first six months, about one in five according to a recent national survey. Interviewing is a skilled process and the aim of this chapter is to help you develop the skills required by first defining the nature of a selection interview and its content and then providing guidance on preparing for and planning the interview, interviewing techniques and assessing the data.

The nature of a selection interview

A selection interview should provide you with the answers to three fundamental questions:

1 Can the individual do the job? Is the person capable of doing the work to the standard required?
2 Will the individual do the job? Is the person well motivated?

3 How is the individual likely to fit into the team? Will I be able to work well with this person?

It should take the form of a conversation with a purpose. It is a conversation because candidates should be given the opportunity to talk freely about themselves and their careers. But the conversation has to be planned, directed and controlled to achieve your aims in the time available.

Your task as an interviewer is to draw candidates out to ensure that you get the information you want. Candidates should be encouraged to do most of the talking – one of the besetting sins of poor interviewers is that they talk too much. But you have to plan the structure of the interview to achieve its purpose and decide in advance the questions you need to ask – questions which will give you what you need to make an accurate assessment.

Overall, an effective approach to interviewing can be summed up as the three Cs:

- Content – the information you want and the questions you ask to get it.
- Contact – your ability to make and maintain good contact with candidates; to establish the sort of rapport that will encourage them to talk freely, thus revealing their strengths and their weaknesses.
- Control – your ability to control the interview so that you get the information you want.

All this requires you to plan the interview thoroughly in terms of content, timing, structure and use of questions.

The content of an interview

The content of an interview can be analysed into three sections; its beginning, middle and end.

Beginning

At the start of the interview you should put candidates at their ease. You want them to talk freely in response to your questions. They won't do this if you plunge in too abruptly. At least welcome them and thank them for coming to the interview, expressing genuine pleasure about the meeting. But don't waste too much time talking about their journey or the weather.

Some interviewers start by describing the company and the job. Wherever possible it is best to eliminate this part of the interview by sending candidates a brief job description and something about the organization.

If you are not careful you will spend far too much time at this stage, especially if the candidate later turns out to be clearly unsuitable. A brief reference to the job should suffice and this can be extended at the end of the interview.

Middle

The middle part of the interview is where you find out what you need to know about candidates. It should take at least 80 per cent of the time, leaving, say, 5 per cent at the beginning and 15 per cent at the end.

This is when you ask questions designed to provide information on:

- the extent to which the knowledge, skills, capabilities and personal qualities of candidates meet the person specification;
- the career history and ambitions of candidates.

End

At the end of the interview you should give candidates the opportunity to ask about the job and the company. How they do this can often give you clues about the degree to which applicants are interested and their ability to ask pertinent questions.

You may want to expand a little on the job if candidates are promising and extol its attractive features. This is fine as long as they are not exaggerated. To give a 'realistic preview', the possible downsides should be mentioned, for example the need to travel or unsocial working hours. If candidates are clearly unsuitable you can tactfully help them to de-select themselves by referring to aspects of the work which may not appeal to them, or for which they are not really qualified. At this stage you should ask final questions about the availability of candidates, as long as they are promising. You can ask when they would be able to start and about any holiday arrangements to which they are committed.

You should also ask their permission to obtain references from their present and previous employers. They might not want you to approach their present employer and in this case you should tell them that if they are made an offer of employment it would be conditional on a satisfactory reference from their employer. It is useful to ensure that you have the names of people you can approach.

Finally, you inform candidates of what happens next. If some time could elapse before they hear from you, they should be told that you will be writing as soon as possible but that there will be some delay (don't make a promise you will be unable to keep).

It is not normally good practice to inform candidates of your decision at the end of the interview. You should take time to reflect on their suitability and you don't want to give them the impression that you are making a snap judgement.

Preparing for the interview

Initial preparations

Your first step in preparing for an interview should be to familiarize or re-familiarize yourself with the person specification which defines the sort of individual you want in terms of qualifications, experience and personality. It is also advisable at this stage to prepare questions which you can put to all candidates to obtain the information you require. If you ask everyone some identical questions you will be able to compare the answers.

You should then read the candidates' CVs and application forms or letters. This will identify any special questions you should ask about their career or, to fill in the gaps, – 'what does this gap between jobs C and D signify?' (although you would not put the question as baldly as that; it would be better to say something like this: 'I see there was a gap of six months between when you left your job in C and started in D. Would you mind telling me what you were doing during this time?').

Timing

You should decide at this stage how long you want to spend on each interview. As a rule of thumb, 45 to 60 minutes are usually required for senior professional or technical appointments. Middle-ranking jobs need about 30 to 45 minutes. The more routine jobs can be covered in 20 to 30 minutes. But the time allowed depends on the job and you do not want to insult a candidate by conducting a superficial interview.

Planning the interview

When planning interviews you should give some thought to how you are going to sequence your questions, especially in the middle part. There are two basic approaches as described below.

Biographical approach

The biographical approach is probably the most popular because it is simple to use and appears to be logical. The interview can be sequenced chronologically, starting with the first job or even before that with school and, if appropriate, college or university. The succeeding jobs, if any, are then dealt with in turn, ending with the present job on which most time is spent if the candidate has been in it for a reasonable time. If you are not careful, however, using the chronological method for someone who has had a number of jobs can mean spending too much time on the earlier jobs, leaving insufficient time for the most important recent experiences.

To overcome this problem, an alternative biographical approach is to start with the present job, which is discussed in some depth. The interviewer then works backwards, job by job, but only concentrating on particularly interesting or relevant experience in earlier jobs.

The problem with the biographical approach is that it is predictable. Experienced candidates are familiar with it and have their story ready, glossing over any weak points. It can also be unreliable. You can easily miss an important piece of information by concentrating on a succession of jobs rather than focusing on key aspects of the candidates' experience that illustrate their capabilities.

Targeted approach

This approach is based on an analysis of the person specification. You can then select the criteria on which you will judge the suitability of the candidate, which will put you in a position to 'target' these key criteria during the interview. You can decide on the questions you need to ask to draw out from candidates information about their knowledge, skills, capabilities and personal qualities, which can be compared with the criteria to assess the extent to which candidates meet the specification. This is probably the best way of focusing your interview to ensure that you get all the information you require about candidates for comparison with the person specification. It can be combined with a biographical approach by ensuring that the targeted information is obtained from a discussion of the candidate's job experience, especially in their more recent jobs.

Interviewing techniques

Questioning

The most important interviewing technique you need to acquire and practise is questioning. Asking pertinent questions that elicit informative responses is a skill that people do not necessarily possess, but it is one they can develop. To improve your questioning techniques it is a good idea at the end of an interview to ask yourself: 'Did I ask the right questions?', 'Did I put them to the candidate well?', 'Did I get candidates to respond freely?'

There are a number of different types of questions as described below. By choosing the right ones you can get candidates to open up or you can pin them down to giving you specific information or to extending or clarifying a reply. The other skills you should possess are establishing rapport, listening, maintaining continuity, keeping contact and note-taking. These are considered later in this section of the chapter.

The main types of questions are described below.

OPEN QUESTIONS

Open questions are the best ones to use to get candidates to talk – to draw them out. These are questions which cannot be answered by a yes or no and which encourage a full response. Single word answers are seldom illuminating. It is a good idea to begin the interview with one or two open questions, thus helping candidates to settle in.

Open-ended questions or phrases inviting a response can be phrased as follows:

- I'd like you to tell me about the sort of work you are doing in your present job.
- What do you know about...?
- Could you give me some examples of...?
- In what ways do you think your experience fits you to do this job?

PROBING QUESTIONS

Probing questions are used to get further details or to ensure that you are getting all the facts. You ask them when answers have been too generalized or when you suspect that there may be some more relevant information, which candidates have not disclosed. A candidate may claim to have done something and it may be useful to find out more about exactly what contribution was made. Poor interviewers tend to let general and uninformative answers pass by without probing for further details, simply because they are sticking rigidly to a pre-determined list of open questions. Skilled interviewers are able to flex their approach to ensure they get the facts while still keeping control to ensure that the interview is completed on time.

The following are some other examples of probing questions:

- You've informed me that you have had experience in... Could you tell me more about what you did?
- Could you describe in more detail the equipment you use?
- What training have you had to operate your machine/equipment/computer?
- Why do you think that happened?

CLOSED QUESTIONS

Closed questions aim to clarify a point of fact. The expected reply will be an explicit single word or brief sentence. In a sense, a closed question acts as a probe but produces a succinct factual statement without going into detail. When you ask a closed question you intend to find out:

- What the candidate has or has not done – 'What did you do then?'
- Why something took place – 'Why did that happen?'
- When something took place – 'When did that happen?'

- How something happened – 'How did that situation arise?'
- Where something happened – 'Where were you at the time?'
- Who took part – 'Who else was involved?'

CAPABILITY QUESTIONS

Capability questions aim to establish what candidates know, the skills they possess and use and what they are capable of doing. They can be open, probing or closed but they will always be focused as precisely as possible on the contents of the person specification referring to knowledge, skills and capabilities.

The sort of capability questions you can ask are:

- What do you know about...?
- How did you gain this knowledge?
- What are the key skills you are expected to use in your work?
- How would your present employer rate the level of skill you have reached in...?

UNHELPFUL QUESTIONS

There are two types of questions that are unhelpful:

- Multiple questions such as 'What skills do you use most frequently in your job? Are they technical skills, leadership skills, teamworking skills or communicating skills?' will only confuse candidates. You will probably get a partial or misleading reply. Ask only one question at a time.
- Leading questions, which indicate the reply you expect, are also unhelpful. If you ask a question such as 'That's what you think, isn't it?' you will get the reply: 'Yes, I do'. If you ask a question such as 'I take it that you don't really believe that...?' You will get the reply: 'No, I don't'. Neither of these replies will get you anywhere.

QUESTIONS TO BE AVOIDED

Avoid any questions that could be construed as being biased on the grounds of sex, race, age or disability.

Ten useful questions

The following are ten useful questions from which you can select any that are particularly relevant:

1 What are the most important aspects of your present job?

2 What do you think have been your most notable achievements in your career to date?

3 What sort of problems have you successfully solved recently in your job?

4 What have you learned from your present job?

5 What has been your experience in...?

6 What do you know about...?

7 What is your approach to handling...?

8 What particularly interests you in this job and why?

9 Now you have heard more about the job, would you please tell me which aspects of your experience are most relevant?

10 Is there anything else about your career that hasn't come out yet in this interview, but that you think I ought to hear?

Assessing the data

If you have carried out a good interview you should have the data to assess the extent to which candidates meet each of the key points in the person specification. You can summarize your assessments by marking candidates against each of the points – 'exceeds specification', 'fully meets specification', 'just meets the minimum specification', 'does not meet the minimum specification'.

You can assess motivation broadly as 'highly motivated, 'reasonably well motivated', 'not very well motivated'.

You should also draw some conclusions from the candidate's career history and the other information you have gained about their behaviour at work. Credit should be given for a career that has progressed steadily, even if there have been several job changes. But a lot of job hopping for no good reason and without making progress can lead you to suspect that a candidate is not particularly stable.

No blame should be attached to a single setback – it can happen to anyone. But if the pattern is repeated you can reasonably be suspicious. Redundancy is not a stigma – it is happening all the time.

Finally, there is the delicate question of whether you think you will be able to work with the candidate, and whether you think he or she will fit into the team. You have to be very careful about making judgements about how you will get on with someone. But if you are absolutely certain that the chemistry will not work, then you have to take account of that feeling, as long as you ensure that you have reasonable grounds for it on the basis of the behaviour of the candidate at the interview. But be aware of the common mistakes that interviewers can make. These include:

- jumping to conclusions on a single piece of favourable evidence – the 'halo effect';

- jumping to conclusions on a single piece of unfavourable evidence – the 'horns effect';

- not weighing up the balance between the favourable and unfavourable evidence logically and objectively;

- coming to firm conclusions on inadequate evidence;

- making snap or hurried judgements;

- making prejudiced judgements on the grounds of sex, race, age, disability, religion, appearance, accent, class or any aspect of the candidate's life history, circumstances or career which do not fit your preconceptions of what you are looking for.

Coming to a conclusion

Compare your assessment of each of the candidates against one another. If any candidate fails in an area which is critical to success, he or she should be rejected. You can't take a chance. Your choice should be made between the candidates who reach an acceptable standard against each of the criteria. You can then come to an overall judgement by reference to their assessments under each heading and their career history as to which one is most likely to succeed.

In the end, your decision between qualified candidates may well be judgemental. There may be one outstanding candidate but quite often there are two or three. In these circumstances you have to come to a balanced view on which one is more likely to fit the job and the organization and have potential for a long-term career, if this is possible. Don't, however, settle for second best in desperation. It is better to try again.

Remember to make and keep notes of the reasons for your choice and why candidates have been rejected. These together with the applications should be kept for at least six months just in case your decision is challenged as being discriminatory.

EXERCISE 11.1

Selection interviewing skills

Name at least six points that someone interviewing a candidate should bear in mind.

SUMMARY POINTS

- As a manager, one of your most important people management tasks will be to interview candidates for a position on
  your team.

- An effective approach to interviewing can be summed up
  as the three Cs: (1) Content – the information you want
  and the questions you ask to get it; (2) Contact – your ability
  to make and maintain good contact with candidates; to
  establish the sort of rapport that will encourage them to talk
  freely, thus revealing their strengths and their weaknesses;
  (3) Control – the degree to which you control the contents
  and timing of the interview overall.

- The content of an interview can be analysed in three
  sections: (1) at the start of the interview you should put
  candidates at ease; (2) the middle part of the interview is
  where you find out what you need to know about candidates;
  (3) the end is when you give candidates the opportunity to
  ask about the job and the company.

- There are two basic approaches to planning interviews:
  (1) in the biographical approach, the interview is sequenced
  chronologically, starting with the first job or even before
  that with school and, if appropriate, college or university.
  The succeeding jobs, if any, are then dealt with in turn ending
  with the present job, on which most time is spent; (2) the
  targeted approach is based on an analysis of the person
  specification from which you select the criteria on which
  you will judge the suitability of the candidate, which will
  put you in a position to 'target' these key criteria during the
  interview.

- The most important interviewing technique you need to acquire and practise is questioning, to establish if the candidate can and will do the job and will fit into the team.
- If you have carried out a good interview, you should have the data to assess the extent to which candidates meet each of the key points in the person specification. You can summarize your assessments by marking candidates against each of the points – 'exceeds specification', 'fully meets specification', 'just meets the minimum specification', 'does not meet the minimum specification'.

12 Helping people to learn and develop

As a manager or team leader you need skilled, knowledgeable and competent people in your department or team. You may appoint able people from within and outside the organization but most of them will still have a lot to learn about their jobs. And to improve your team members' performance you must not only ensure that they learn the basic skills they need but also that they develop those skills to enable them to perform even better when faced with new demands and challenges.

Most learning happens informally at the place of work although it can be supplemented by such activities as e-learning (the delivery of learning opportunities and support via computer, networked and web-based technology) and formal 'off-the-job' training courses. It is your job to ensure that favourable conditions for learning 'on the job' exist generally in your area as well as taking steps to help individuals develop.

How you can promote learning and development

Overall your role is to ensure that conditions in your department or team are conducive to learning. This can be described as creating a 'learning culture', an environment in which steps are taken to understand how learning can benefit individual and team performance, to provide learning opportunities as the need arises, to encourage self-managed learning and to recognize that learning is a continuous process in which all can take part and everyone can benefit. Your function is to provide the leadership and example that will foster this culture and to see that guidance and help are available from you and others to promote learning and development. To do this you must understand learning needs, provide for induction training, use day-to-day contacts with people to provide them with learning opportunities, and prepare and agree learning contracts and personal development plans. You must also be familiar with the various techniques or processes involved, namely coaching, mentoring and job instruction.

Understanding learning needs

You should be aware of the knowledge and skills required to carry out each job in your team so that you can plan the learning programme required for new team members and review the levels reached by existing team members to identify any further learning needs. The basis for this should be role profiles which spell out the knowledge and skills required to reach an acceptable level of performance.

Induction training

You are initially involved in helping people to learn every time you welcome new members of your team, plan how they are going to acquire the know-how required (preferably as recorded in a learning specification), provide for them to receive systematic guidance and instruction on the tasks they have to carry out, and see that the plan is implemented. As a manager you may delegate the responsibility for providing this induction training to a team leader, or as a team leader you may carry it out yourself – the ideal method – or delegate it to a team member. Whichever approach you use you should be confident that the individual responsible for the induction has the right temperament and skills to do it. This includes being aware of the conditions required for effective learning as set out earlier and of the use of coaching, mentoring and job instruction as described later.

Continuous learning

You provide learning opportunities for team members every time you delegate tasks to them. At the briefing stage you ensure that they are fully aware of what they have to do and have the knowledge and skills to do it. If appropriate, you ask them to tell you what they need to know and be able to do to carry out the task. If you are unsure that they have all the skills required but still believe that they can do it with additional guidance or help, then this is what you provide yourself or arrange for someone else to do so.

As you monitor progress to whatever degree is necessary (for some people you will just let them get on with it; for less experienced people you might need to monitor more closely), you can follow up to find out if the best approach is being used and if not, give them any further help they need. But you must be careful. People will not learn if you do it all for them. You have to give them a chance to find things out for themselves and even make mistakes as long as things are not going badly wrong.

When you review outcomes with people, preferably immediately after the event, it is a good idea to ask them what they have learned so that it is reinforced for future use. You can also ask them if their experience has shown that they need to learn. This is a good opportunity for you to get individuals to develop their own learning plans (self-managed learning) but it also means that you can step in and offer your support.

Personal development planning

Personal development planning is carried out by individuals with guidance, encouragement and help from you as required. A personal development plan sets out the actions people propose to take to learn and to develop themselves. They take responsibility for formulating and implementing the plan but they receive support from their managers in doing so.

The stages of personal development planning are modelled in Figure 12.1:

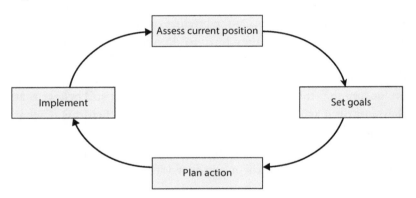

FIGURE 12.1 Stages in preparing and implementing a personal development plan

Coaching

Coaching is a one-to-one method of helping people develop their skills and competences. Coaching is often provided by specialists from inside or outside the organization who concentrate on specific areas of skills or behaviour, for example leadership. But it is also something that can happen in the workplace. As a manager or team leader you should be prepared and able to act as a coach when necessary to see that learning takes place.

The need for coaching may arise from formal or informal performance reviews, but opportunities for coaching emerge during day-to-day activities. As part of the normal process of management, coaching consists of:

- making people aware of how well they are performing by, for example, asking them questions to establish the extent to which they have thought through what they are doing;
- controlled delegation – ensuring that individuals not only know what is expected of them but also understand what they need to know and be able to do to complete the task satisfactorily; this gives managers an opportunity to provide guidance at the outset, as guidance at a later stage may be seen as interference;
- using whatever situations that may arise as opportunities to promote learning;
- encouraging people to look at higher-level problems and how they would tackle them.

To succeed in coaching you need to understand that your role is to help people to learn and see that they are motivated to learn. They should be aware that their present level of knowledge or skill or their behaviour needs to be improved if they are going to perform their work satisfactorily. Individuals should be given guidance on what they should be learning and feedback on how they are doing, and, because learning is an active not a passive process, they should be actively involved with you in your role as a coach who should be constructive, building on strengths and experience.

Coaching may be informal but it has to be planned. It is not simply checking from time to time on what people are doing and then advising them on how to do it better. Nor is it occasionally telling people where they have gone wrong and throwing in a lecture for good measure. As far as possible, coaching should take place within the framework of a general plan of the areas and direction in which individuals will benefit from further development. Coaching plans can and should be incorporated into the personal development plans set out in a performance agreement.

Coaching should provide motivation, structure and effective feedback. As a coach, you should believe that people can succeed and that they can contribute to their own success. The following criteria for evaluating the performance of a coach were listed by Gray (2010):

- establishes rapport;
- creates trust and respect;
- demonstrates effective communication skills;
- promotes self-awareness and self-knowledge;
- uses active listening and questioning techniques;
- assists goal development and setting;
- motivates;
- encourages alternative perspectives;
- assists in making sense of a situation;
- identifies significant patterns of thinking and behaving;
- provides an appropriate mix of challenge and support;
- facilitates depth of understanding;
- shows compassion;
- acts ethically;
- inspires curiosity;
- acts as a role model;
- values diversity and difference;
- promotes action and reflection.

Mentoring

As a manager you may be asked to act as a mentor and you should receive guidance on what is involved. Mentoring is the process of using specially selected and trained individuals to provide guidance, pragmatic advice and continuing support, which will help the person or persons allocated to them to learn and develop. It can be regarded as a method of helping people to learn as distinct from coaching, which is a relatively directive means of increasing people's competence.

Mentoring involves learning on the job, which must always be the best way of acquiring the particular skills and knowledge the job holder needs. It also complements formal training by providing those who benefit from it with individual guidance from experienced managers who are 'wise in the ways of the organization'.

Mentors provide people with:

- advice in drawing up self-development programmes or learning contracts;
- general help with learning programmes;
- guidance on how to acquire the necessary knowledge and skills to do a new job;
- advice on dealing with any administrative, technical or people problems individuals meet, especially in the early stages of their careers;
- information on 'the way things are done around here' – the corporate culture in terms of expected behaviour;
- coaching in specific skills;
- help in tackling projects – not by doing it for them but by pointing them in the right direction; helping people to help themselves;
- a parental figure with whom individuals can discuss their aspirations and concerns and who will lend a sympathetic ear to their problems.

Mentors need to give the right non-directive but supportive help to the person or persons they are dealing with. They must therefore be carefully briefed and trained in their role.

But you may be able to call on an organizational mentor to provide help with an individual in your area.

A version of mentoring which you can use within your department is what in the United States is sometimes called 'buddying'. This involves appointing someone in your department or team to look after newcomers and ensure that they get the guidance and help they need to settle down quickly.

Job instruction

When you arrange for people to learn specific tasks, the learning will be more effective if you use or arrange for someone to use job instruction techniques. The sequence of instruction should consist of the following stages.

PREPARATION

Preparation means that the trainer must have a plan for presenting the subject matter and using appropriate teaching methods, visual aids and demonstration aids. It also means preparing trainees for the instruction that is to follow. They should want to learn. They must perceive that the learning will be relevant and useful to them personally. They should be encouraged to take pride in their job and to appreciate the satisfaction that comes from skilled performance.

PRESENTATION

Presentation should consist of a combination of telling and showing – explanation and demonstration. Explanation should be as simple and direct as possible: the trainer explains briefly the ground to be covered and what to look for. He or she makes the maximum use of charts, diagrams, and other visual aids. The aim should be to teach first things first and then proceed from the known to the unknown, the simple to the complex, the concrete to the abstract, the general to the particular, the observation to reasoning, and the whole to the parts and back to the whole again.

DEMONSTRATION

Demonstration is an essential stage in instruction, especially when the skill to be learned is mainly a doing skill. Demonstration can take place in three stages:

1 The complete operation is shown at normal speed to show the trainee how the task should be carried out eventually.

2 The operation is demonstrated slowly and in correct sequence, element by element, to indicate clearly what is done and the order in which each task is carried out.

3 The operation is demonstrated again slowly, at least two or three times, to stress the how, when and why of successive movements.

The learner then practices by imitating the instructor and constantly repeating the operation under guidance. The aim is to reach the target level of performance for each element of the total task, but the instructor must constantly strive to develop coordinated and integrated performance; the smooth combination of the separate elements of the task into a whole job pattern.

FOLLOW-UP

Follow-up continues during the training period for all the time required by the learner to reach the desired level of performance in terms of quality, speed and attention to safety. During the follow-up stage, the learner will continue to need help with particularly difficult tasks or to overcome temporary setbacks that could result in a deterioration of performance. The instructor may have to repeat the presentation of the elements and supervise practice more closely until the trainee regains confidence or masters the task.

EXERCISE 12.1

What managers can do about learning and development
List at least three things a manager can do to promote learning and development.

SUMMARY POINTS

- As a manager or team leader you need skilled, knowledgeable and competent people in your department or team.
- Most learning happens informally at the place of work.
- Your role is to ensure that conditions in your department or team are conducive to learning.
- You should be aware of the knowledge and skills required to carry out each job in your team so that you can plan the learning programme required for new team members and review the levels reached by existing team members to identify any further learning needs.
- You provide learning opportunities for team members every time you delegate tasks to them.
- Personal development planning is carried out by individuals with guidance, encouragement and help from you as required. A personal development plan sets out the actions people propose to take to learn and to develop themselves.
- You are initially involved in helping people to learn every time you welcome new members of your team, plan how they are going to acquire the know-how required (preferably as recorded in a learning specification), provide for them to receive systematic guidance and instruction on the tasks they have to carry out, and see that the plan is implemented.

- Coaching is a one-to-one method of helping people develop their skills and competences. As part of the normal process of management, coaching consists of making people aware of how well they are performing, controlling delegation using whatever situations which may arise as opportunities to promote learning, and encouraging people to look at higher-level problems and how they would tackle them.

- As a manager you may be asked to act as a mentor and you should receive guidance on what is involved.

- Mentoring is the process of using specially selected and trained individuals to provide guidance, pragmatic advice and continuing support, which will help the person or persons allocated to them to learn and develop.

- When you arrange for people to learn specific tasks, especially those involving manual skills, the learning will be more effective if you use or arrange for someone to use job instruction techniques. The sequence of instruction should consist of the following stages: preparation, presentation, demonstration and follow-up.

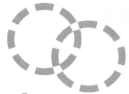

13 Rewarding people

People will contribute more and cooperate more wholeheartedly if they feel that they are valued. This happens when you recognize them for what they achieve and reward them according to their contribution. Although many organizations have some form of reward system, usually managed by the HR function, it is the front-line manager who exerts the greatest influence on how people are valued. The extent to which line managers are responsible for rewarding people varies according to the system used or the lack of a system. Managers in public and many voluntary sector organizations exert little influence on the financial aspects of reward. There will be a pay spine with fixed increments related to service and, probably, a job evaluation scheme which dictates job gradings and therefore pay. However, in many small or even medium-sized organizations there is no formal reward system and managers have a considerable degree of freedom in managing pay.

Reference has been made above to 'reward systems' and if you are working in an organization with one, it is necessary to understand what this term means; this is explained in the first part of the chapter. The overall approach you should adopt to rewarding people, whether or not there is a system, is discussed in the next part. The following parts of the chapter are concerned with what managers and team leaders do about deciding on grades and rates for the job, and with conducting pay reviews when systems exist for progressing pay according to performance or contribution. The last part of the chapter covers what managers do when there is no reward system or at least only a vestigial one.

Reward systems

A reward system consists of explicit policies, practices and procedures which are organized and managed as a whole. A complete system is based on reward policies, which set guidelines for decision making and action. For example, an organization may have a policy which sets the levels of pay compared with average market rates. The system itself consists of reward practices which comprise grading jobs, deciding on rates of pay and reviewing pay levels, grade and pay structures, methods of progressing pay according to performance, contribution or service, and employee benefits such as pension schemes and sick pay. The degree to which these practices are formalized will vary considerably between different organizations. For example many organizations (60 per cent according to a recent survey) have formal job evaluation schemes, but a large proportion rely on more or less informal methods. Similarly, a lot of organizations have formal grade and pay structures but 20 per cent of those responding to the survey had no structure at all. And performance pay schemes vary enormously in the ways in which they operate.

The implication is that if you want to play your part in managing the reward system you must understand how it works. You should be told this by HR but if not, it's up to you to find out.

Approaches to rewarding people

You need to understand the factors that determine the effectiveness of the formal or informal system in terms of the degree to which it satisfies people because they feel valued and the extent to which it contributes to their motivation and engagement. These factors consist of the use of both financial and non-financial rewards and how the system is operated as a fair, equitable, consistent and transparent approach to rewarding people.

Financial and non-financial rewards

Financial rewards consist of the rate for the job (base pay), pay related to performance or contribution (merit pay) and benefits such as pension schemes. The ways financial rewards work as motivators were considered in Chapter 4. To be effective such rewards should be perceived as fair, equitable and consistent. They will work better if the system is transparent. People should also expect that their efforts will lead to a worthwhile reward – there must be a 'line of sight' between what they do and what they get, between the effort and the reward. They will also respond more to financial rewards if the system is transparent – they know how it works and how it affects them.

Non-financial rewards can provide a better basis for valuing people because they are more under your control. Financial rewards are restricted by budgets and company procedures. The main ways of valuing people through non-financial rewards are:

- providing them with the opportunity to achieve;
- recognizing their contribution by praise and by 'applause' (letting others know how well you value an individual);
- giving people more responsibility (empowering them);
- providing them with the opportunity to grow – offering learning opportunities, encouraging and supporting the preparation and implementation of personal development plans and broadening their experience (job enlargement).

Both financial and non-financial rewards are important. Many organizations are now combining their impact by developing what is called a 'total rewards' system. Essentially, this says that there is more to rewarding people than throwing money at them. Total rewards encompass all the elements that make it worthwhile for people to come to work. Perhaps the most powerful argument for a total rewards approach was produced by Professor Jeffrey Pfeffer of Stanford University (1998):

> *Creating a fun, challenging, and empowered work environment in which individuals are able to use their abilities to do meaningful jobs for which they are shown appreciation is likely to be a more certain way to enhance motivation and performance – even though creating such an environment may be more difficult and take more time than simply turning the reward lever.*

Fixing grades and rates of pay

If there is a grade and pay structure, those parts of the organization's reward system in the form of its job evaluation scheme and its procedures for analysing market rates largely determine how jobs are graded and the basic rates for jobs. You can influence decisions about individuals by invoking the job evaluation scheme to grade or re-grade jobs and by scanning any information on market rates which you think justifies more pay for someone.

Job evaluation procedures are based on job descriptions, which highlight the characteristics of the job with respect to any factors used in the scheme such as the levels of skill and responsibility involved. In point-factor schemes (the most common method) judgements about these levels are converted into points so that a total score is attached to a job, which determines its grade, and therefore pay. Managers are often tempted to advance the cause of their staff by inflating the characteristics set out in the job description and therefore committing the sin of 'point grabbing'. This is undesirable because (a) it is dishonest, (b) it damages the integrity of the scheme, and (c) it creates inequities between jobs.

One of the issues that should concern you is that of equal pay for work of equal value. Your aim should be to achieve equity between like jobs held by men or women, people of different racial groups, sexual orientation or religion, people with and without disabilities and older and younger people. This will avoid expensive and time-consuming equal pay cases but, more importantly, it is the right thing to do.

Reviewing pay

Decisions on general 'across the board' increases are generally outside the line manager's control. But if your organization has a scheme for relating individual pay to performance you will be involved in determining the amounts people should get. In the past, line managers were often given little scope to make such decisions and even the extent to which they could influence them was limited. Increasingly, however, responsibility is being devolved to managers and this makes quite considerable demands on their judgement and their ability to be fair and consistent. One of the reasons why most unions in the UK oppose performance-related pay is that they believe, not without some justification, that managers tend to be unfair and prone to prejudice and favouritism when, as part of a performance appraisal scheme, they rate performance on a scale which governs pay increases. Managers can also subvert the system by awarding a few high increases to their favourites and keeping within their budgets by distributing small awards or nothing at all to other people. Alternatively, they can fail to discriminate between performance levels by awarding everyone, or at least the vast majority of people, the same.

Some organizations have addressed these issues by providing managers with guidelines and technical support in making pay decisions. Typically, the guidelines suggest that in making pay decisions managers should consider:

- the individual's current role and pay position in the salary range;
- what people in the same or similar roles are being paid;
- how they value the individual's performance in this role;
- the market rate for the role.

Many organizations try to avoid the problems of relying on performance ratings in the annual performance review to inform pay decisions, largely because this process runs counter to the main objective of these reviews, which is to improve performance and to provide the basis for development plans. Quite often, such organizations 'decouple' pay reviews from performance reviews, ie they hold them at separate times in the year, possibly three or four months apart. They may even abandon ratings altogether and simply ask managers to recommend above average, average or below average pay increases depending on their assessments of contribution, potential market rate relativities and the rates of pay of other team members. To help managers they may provide them with systems support.

Managing without a reward system

If you do not have the support of a formal reward system or a helpful HR department, you may largely have to make decisions yourself on what people should be paid. You may have to get approval from a higher authority and you may have to work within a budget, but you are virtually on your own when you deal with your staff. In these circumstances there are 10 things you should do as set out below.

TEN WAYS TO MANAGE YOUR OWN REWARD SYSTEM

1 Remember that you are attempting to achieve internal equity (paying people according to their relative contribution) at the same time as being externally competitive (paying rates that will attract and retain the level of people you need).

2 Appreciate that it is often difficult to reconcile equity and competitiveness.

3 Obtain information on market rates from reliable sources (surveys and agencies). Do not rely on job advertisements.

4 If you have to bow to market forces make certain that you have got your facts right and that the case for what is sometimes called a market supplement can be objectively justified.

5 Take steps to ensure that equal pay is provided for work of equal value.

6 Try to obtain objective reasons for differentiating between the base pay of different jobs. While you need not go to the extreme of developing your own analytical job evaluation scheme, you can at least compare jobs by reference to role profiles, which indicate the levels of responsibility and knowledge and skills they involve.

7 Review basic rates of pay by reference to market rates, not just to increases in the cost of living.

8 When looking at individual rates of pay consider what people are earning in relation to their colleagues. Ask yourself the questions: are they just as good, are they better, are they worse than their colleagues? Rank your team members in order by reference to their relative levels of contribution. Give the top 15 per cent or so an above-average increase, the bottom 15 per cent or so a below-average increase and the rest an average increase.

9 Consider other methods of rewarding your people besides pay, especially recognizing their contribution.

10 Ensure that your team members know the basis upon which you have made decisions about their pay and give them the opportunity to raise any of their concerns.

EXERCISE 13.1

Managing performance-related pay
If your organization introduced performance-related pay for the first time, what should you do to make it a success?

SUMMARY POINTS

- People will contribute more and cooperate more whole-heartedly if they feel that they are valued.

- This happens when you recognize them for what they achieve and reward them according to their contribution.

- A reward system consists of explicit policies, practices and procedures, which are organized and managed as a whole.

- Financial rewards consist of the rate for the job (base pay), pay related to performance or contribution (merit pay) and benefits such as pension schemes.

- Non-financial rewards can provide a better basis for valuing people because they are more under your control. They include recognizing their contribution, providing them with the opportunity to achieve and grow; and giving them more responsibility.

- If there is a grade and pay structure, those parts of the organization's reward system in the form of its job evaluation scheme and its procedures for analysing market rates largely determine how jobs are graded and the basic rates for jobs. If your organization has a scheme for relating individual pay to performance you will be involved in determining the amounts people should get.

14 Managing change

Change is the only constant thing that happens in organizations. There can be few managers who have never had to meet the challenge of introducing a new organization structure, new methods of working, a revision to job duties, new management systems or alterations in terms and conditions of employment.

The challenge arises because people can find change difficult to accept or to cope with. Many people resist change, any change. Some may accept the need for change but can't adjust their behaviour to respond to it. There are some people who welcome change but they are probably in the minority.

Your role as a manager is to see that change happens smoothly when the occasion arises. To do this you should know about the process of change, the reasons why people resist change and how to overcome this resistance, and the specific steps you can take to introduce change and ensure that it takes place as planned.

The change process

Conceptually, the change process starts with an awareness of the need for change. An analysis of this situation and the factors that have created it leads to a diagnosis of their distinctive characteristics and an indication of the direction in which action needs to be taken. Possible courses of action can next be identified and evaluated and a choice made of the preferred action. It is then necessary to decide how to get from here to there. Managing change during this transition state is a critical phase in the change process. It is here that the problems of introducing change emerge and have to be managed. These problems can include resistance to change, instability, high levels of stress, misdirected energy, conflict and loss of momentum. Hence the need to do everything possible to anticipate reactions and likely impediments to the introduction of change.

The final stage in which the new structure, system or process is installed can also be demanding, indeed painful. As described by Pettigrew and Whipp (1991), the implementation of change is an 'iterative, cumulative and reformulation-in-use process'.

The next issue is how to 'hold the gains', ie how to ensure that the change is embedded and maintained. This means continuously monitoring the effects and impact of the change and taking corrective action where necessary to ensure that it continues to work well.

Resistance to change

Change management programmes have to take account of the fact that many people resist change. There are those who are stimulated by change and see it as a challenge and an opportunity. But they are in the minority. It is always easy for people to select any of the following ten reasons for doing nothing:

1 It won't work.

2 We're already doing it.

3 It's been tried before without success.

4 It's not practical.

5 It won't solve the problem.

6 It's too risky.

7 It's based on pure theory.

8 It will cost too much.

9 It will antagonize the customers / management / the union / the workers / the shareholders.

10 It will create more problems than it solves.

Reasons for resistance to change

People resist change when they see it as a threat to their established life at work. They are used to their routines and patterns of behaviour and may be concerned about their ability to cope with new demands. They see change as a threat to familiar patterns of behaviour. They may believe that it will affect their status, security or their earnings. Sometimes, and with good reason, they may not believe statements by management that the change is for their benefit as well as that of the organization. They may feel that managements have ulterior motives and sometimes, the louder management protests, the less it will be believed.

Overcoming resistance to change

Because resistance to change is a natural and even inevitable phenomenon it may be difficult to overcome. But the attempt must be made. This starts with an analysis of the likely effect on change and the extent to which it might be resisted, by whom and why. It is not enough to think out what the change will be and calculate the benefits and costs from the proposer's point of view. The others involved will almost inevitably see the benefits as less and the costs as greater. It is necessary to 'think through' the proposed change and obtain answers to the following questions:

- Will the change alter job content?
- Will it introduce new and unknown tasks?
- Will it disrupt established methods of working?
- Will it rearrange team relationships?
- Will it reduce autonomy or authority?

- Will it be perceived as lowering status?
- Will it lead to job losses?
- Will it result in a loss of pay or other benefits?

It is also necessary to answer the question, 'What are the benefits in pay, status, job satisfaction and career prospects which are generated by the change as well as the increase in performance?'

Resistance to change may never be overcome completely but it can be reduced through involvement and communications.

Involvement

Involvement in the change process gives people the chance to raise and resolve their concerns and make suggestions about the form of the change and how it should be introduced. The aim is to get 'ownership' – a feeling amongst people that the change is something that they are happy to live with because they have been involved in its planning and introduction – it has become their change. People accept what they help to create.

Communicating plans for change

The first and most critical step for managing change is to develop and communicate a clear image of the future. Resistance and confusion frequently develop because people are unclear about what the future state will be like. Thus the purposes of the change become blurred, and individual expectancies are formed on the basis of incorrect information.

Communications should describe why change is necessary, what the changes will look like, how they will be achieved and how people will be affected by them. The aim is to ensure that unnecessary fears are allayed by keeping people informed using a variety of methods – written communications, the intranet and, best of all, face-to-face briefings and discussions.

TEN GUIDELINES FOR CHANGE MANAGEMENT

1 The achievement of sustainable change requires strong commitment and visionary leadership.

2 Proposals for change should be based on a convincing business case supported by a practical programme for implementing the change and reaping the benefits.

3 Change is inevitable and necessary. It is necessary to explain why change is essential and how it will affect everyone.

4 Hard evidence and data on the need for change are the most powerful tools for its achievement, but establishing the need for change is easier than deciding how to satisfy it.

5 People support what they help to create. Commitment to change is improved if those affected by change are allowed to participate as fully as possible in planning and implementing it. The aim should be to get them to 'own' the change as something they want and will be glad to live with.

6 Change will always involve failure as well as success. The failures must be expected and learned from.

7 It is easier to change behaviour by changing processes, structure and systems than to change attitudes.

8 There are always people in organizations who can act as champions of change. They will welcome the challenges and opportunities that change can provide. They are the ones to be chosen as change agents.

9 Resistance to change is inevitable if the individuals concerned feel that they are going to be worse off – implicitly or explicitly. The inept management of change will produce that reaction.

10 Every effort must be made to protect the interests of those affected by change.

EXERCISE 14.1

Managing change

You have to introduce a major change in the working methods of your department which has a staff of 25 people mainly engaged in routine administrative activities. The change will include the introduction of a new computer system and a considerable redistribution of work around the department. Four or five employees will be surplus to requirements.

How do you plan the change?

SUMMARY POINTS

- Change is the only constant thing that happens in organizations.
- The challenge arises because people can find change difficult to accept or to cope with.
- The change process consists of:
    - an awareness of the need for change;
    - a diagnosis of the distinctive characteristics of the change and an indication of the direction in which action needs to be taken;
    - the identification of possible courses of action and the choice of the preferred action;
    - a decision on how to get from here to there (managing the transition);
    - implementing the change.
- People resist change when they see it as a threat to familiar patterns of behaviour. They may believe that it will affect their status, security or their earnings.
- Resistance to change may never be overcome completely but it can be reduced through involvement and communications.

15 Managing conflict

Conflict is inevitable in organizations because they function by means of adjustments and compromises among competitive elements in their structure and membership. Conflict also arises when there is change, because it may be seen as a threat to be challenged or resisted, or when there is frustration – this may produce an aggressive reaction; fight rather than flight.

Conflict is not always to be deplored. It may result from progress and change and it can be used constructively. Bland agreement on everything would be unnatural and enervating. There should be clashes of ideas about tasks and projects, and disagreements should not be suppressed. They should come out into the open because that is the only way to ensure that the issues are explored and conflicts are resolved.

There is such a thing as creative conflict – new or modified ideas, insights, approaches and solutions can be generated by a joint re-examination of different points of view as long as this is based on an objective and rational exchange of information and opinions. But conflict becomes counterproductive when it is based on personality clashes, or when it is treated as an unseemly mess to be hurriedly cleared away, rather than as a problem to be worked through. Conflict management resolution deals with ways of settling differences between groups and handling interpersonal conflicts between individuals.

Handling intergroup conflict

There are three principal ways of resolving intergroup conflict: peaceful coexistence, compromise and problem solving.

Peaceful coexistence

The aim here is to smooth out differences and emphasize the common ground. People are encouraged to learn to live together, there is a good deal of information, contact and exchange of views, and individuals move freely between groups (for example, between headquarters and the field, or between sales and marketing).

This is a pleasant ideal, but it may not be practicable in many situations. There is much evidence that conflict is not necessarily resolved by bringing people together. Improved communications and techniques such as briefing groups may appear to be good ideas but are useless if management has nothing to say that people want to hear. There is also the danger that the real issues, submerged for the moment in an atmosphere of superficial bonhomie, will surface again later.

Compromise

The issue is resolved by negotiation or bargaining and neither party wins or loses. This concept of splitting the difference is essentially pessimistic. The hallmark of this approach is that there is no 'right' or 'best' answer. Agreements only accommodate differences. Real issues are not likely to be solved.

Problem solving

An attempt is made to find a genuine solution to the problem rather than just accommodating different points of view. This is where the apparent paradox of 'creative conflict' comes in. Conflict situations can be used to advantage in order to create better solutions.

If solutions are to be developed by problem solving, they have to be generated by those who share the responsibility for seeing that the solutions work. The sequence of actions is: first, those concerned work to define the problem and agree on the objectives to be attained in reaching a solution, second, the group develops alternative solutions and debates their merits, and third, agreement is reached on the preferred course of action and how it should be implemented.

Handling interpersonal conflict

Handling conflict between individuals can be even more difficult than resolving conflicts between groups. Whether the conflict is openly hostile or subtly covert, strong personal feelings may be involved. However, interpersonal conflict, like intergroup conflict, is an organizational reality which is not necessarily good or bad. It can be destructive, but it can also play a productive role. The approaches to dealing with it are withdrawal, smoothing over differences, reaching a compromise, counselling and constructive confrontation.

Withdrawal

The reaction to interpersonal conflict may be the withdrawal of either party, leaving the other one to hold the field. This is the classic win/lose situation. The problem has been resolved by force, but this may not be the best solution if it represents one person's point of view which has ignored counter-arguments, and has, in fact, steamrollered over them. The winner may be triumphant but the loser will be aggrieved and either demotivated or resolved to fight again another day. There will have been a lull in, but not an end to, the conflict.

Smoothing over differences

Another approach is to smooth over differences and pretend that the conflict does not exist, although no attempt has been made to tackle the root causes. Again, this is an unsatisfactory solution. The issue is likely to re-emerge and the battle will recommence.

Compromise

Yet another approach is bargaining to reach a compromise. This means that both sides are prepared to lose as well as win some points and the aim is to reach a solution acceptable to both sides. Bargaining, however, involves all sorts of tactical and often counter-productive games, and the parties are often more anxious to seek acceptable compromises than to achieve sound solutions.

Counselling

Personal counselling is an approach which does not address the conflict itself but focuses on how the two people are reacting. It gives people a chance to release pent-up tensions and may encourage them to think about new ways of resolving the conflict. But it does not address the essential nature of the conflict, which is the relationship between two people. That is why constructive confrontation offers the best hope of a long-term solution.

Constructive confrontation

Constructive confrontation is a method of bringing the individuals in conflict together with a third party whose function is to help build an exploratory and cooperative climate. Constructive confrontation aims to get the parties involved to understand and explore the other's perceptions and feelings. It is a process of developing mutual understanding to produce a win/win situation. The issues will be confronted but on the basis of a joint analysis, with the help of the third party, of facts relating to the situation and the actual behaviour of those involved. Feelings will be expressed but they will be analysed by reference to specific events and behaviours rather than inferences or speculations about motives. Third parties have a key role in this process, and it is not an easy one. They have to get agreement on the ground rules for discussions aimed at bringing out the facts and minimizing hostile behaviour. They must monitor the ways in which negative feelings are expressed and encourage the parties to produce new definitions of the problem and its cause or causes and new motives to reach a common solution. Third parties must avoid the temptation to support or appear to support either of those in contention. They should adopt a counselling approach, as follows:

- listen actively;
- observe as well as listen;
- help people to understand and define the problem by asking pertinent, open-ended questions;
- recognize feelings and allow them to be expressed;
- help people to define problems for themselves;
- encourage people to explore alternative solutions;
- get people to develop their own implementation plans but provide advice and help if asked.

To conclude, conflict, as has been said, is in itself not to be deplored: it is an inevitable concomitant of progress and change. What is regrettable is the failure to use conflict constructively. Effective problem solving and constructive confrontation both resolve conflicts and open up channels of discussion and cooperative action.

EXERCISE 15.1

Managing conflict

In your department you have two team leaders who strongly disagree about who should be responsible for a particularly interesting and rewarding aspect of the work of the department. They each think that the work would fit best within their remit and that they and their team are best qualified to do it. The argument is becoming increasingly strident and disruptive. Both leaders have strong characters and may find it hard to concede the issue. You think there are strong arguments on both sides and have your own views on what is best. But these team leaders are valuable members of your department and you don't want to upset them by imposing a solution unless that is unavoidable.

How do you tackle this situation?

SUMMARY POINTS

- Conflict is inevitable in organizations because they function by means of adjustments and compromises among competitive elements in their structure and membership.

- There are three principal ways of resolving intergroup conflict: peaceful coexistence, compromise and problem solving.

- The approaches to dealing with interpersonal conflict are withdrawal, smoothing over differences, reaching a compromise, counselling and constructive confrontation.

16 Handling people problems

If you manage people you will have people problems. They are bound to happen and you are the person on the spot who has to handle them. The basic approach you should use in tackling people problems is to:

1 Get the facts. Make sure that you have all the information or evidence you need to understand exactly what the problem is.

2 Weigh and decide. Analyse the facts to identify the causes of the problem. Consider any alternative solutions to the problem and decide which is likely to be the most successful.

3 Take action. Following the decision plan what you are going to do, establish goals and success criteria and put the plan into effect.

4 Check results. Monitor the implementation of the plan and check that the expected results have been obtained.

The most common problems covered in this chapter are to do with:

- disciplinary issues;
- negative behaviour;
- under-performance;
- absenteeism;
- timekeeping;
- handling challenging conversations.

Disciplinary issues

Employees can be dismissed because they are not capable of doing the work or for misconduct. It is normal to go through a formal disciplinary procedure containing staged warnings but instant dismissal can be justified for gross misconduct (eg serious theft) which should preferably be defined in the company's disciplinary procedure or employee handbook. But anyone in the UK with two years' service or more can claim unfair dismissal if their employer cannot show that one of these reasons applied, if the dismissal was not reasonable in the circumstances, if a constructive dismissal has taken place, or if there has been a breach of a customary or agreed redundancy procedure and there are no valid reasons for departing from that procedure.

Even if the employer can prove to an employment tribunal that there was good reason to dismiss the employee the tribunal will still have to decide whether or not the employer acted in a reasonable way at the time of dismissal. The principles defining 'reasonable' behaviour are in line with the principles of natural justice and are as follows:

- the employee should be informed of the nature of the complaint;
- the employee should be given the chance to explain;
- the employee should be given the opportunity to improve, except in particularly gross cases of incapability or misconduct;
- the employee should be warned of the consequences in the shape of dismissal if specified improvements do not take place;
- the employer's decision to dismiss should be based on sufficient evidence;
- the employer should take any mitigating circumstances into account;
- the offence or misbehaviour should merit the penalty of dismissal rather than some lesser penalty.

Your organization may have a statutory disciplinary procedure. You need to know what that procedure is and the part you are expected to play in implementing it. Whether or not there is a formal procedure, if you believe that disciplinary action is necessary you need to take the following steps when planning and conducting a disciplinary interview:

1 Get all the facts in advance, including statements from people involved.

2 Invite the employee to the meeting in writing, explaining why it is being held and that they have the right to have someone present at the meeting on their behalf.

3 Ensure that the employee has reasonable notice (ideally at least two days).

4 Plan how you will conduct the meeting.

5 Line up another member of management to attend the meeting with you to take notes (they can be important if there is an appeal) and generally provide support.

6 Start the interview by stating the complaint to the employee and referring to the evidence.

7 Give the employee plenty of time to respond and state their case.

8 Take a break as required to consider the points raised and to relieve any pressure taking place in the meeting.

9 Consider what action is appropriate, if any. Actions should be staged starting with a recorded written warning, followed, if the problem continues, by a first written warning, then a final written warning and lastly, if the earlier stages have been exhausted, disciplinary action, which would be dismissal in serious cases.

10 Deliver the decision, explaining why it has been taken and confirm it in writing.

If all the stages in the disciplinary procedure have been completed and the employee has to be dismissed, or where immediate dismissal can be justified on the grounds of gross misconduct, you may have to carry out the unpleasant duty of dismissing the employee. Again, you should have a colleague or someone from HR with you when you do this. You should:

- if possible, meet when the office is quiet, preferably on a Friday;
- keep the meeting formal and organized;
- write down what you are going to say in advance, giving the reason and getting your facts, dates and figures right;
- be polite but firm – read out what you have written down and make it clear that it is not open for discussion;
- ensure that the employee clears his or her desk and has no opportunity to take away confidential material or use their computer;
- see the employee off the premises – some companies use security guards as escorts but this is rather heavy handed although it might be useful to have someone on call in case of difficulties.

Handling negative behaviour

You may well come across negative behaviour from time to time on the part of one of the members of your team. This may take the form of lack of interest in the work, unwillingness to cooperate with you or other people, complaining about the work or working conditions, grumbling at being asked to carry out a perfectly reasonable task, objecting strongly to being asked to do something extra (or even refusing to do it) – 'it's not in my job description' – or, in extreme cases, insolence. People exhibiting negative behaviour may be quietly resentful rather than openly disruptive. They mutter away in the background at meetings and lack enthusiasm.

As a manager you can tolerate a certain amount of negative behaviour as long as the individual works reasonably well and does not upset other team members. You have simply to say to yourself 'It takes all sorts...' and put up with it, although you might quietly say during a review meeting 'You're doing a good job but...' If, however, you do take this line you have to be specific. You must cite actual instances. It is no good making generalized accusations which will either be openly refuted or internalized by the receiver, making him or her even more resentful.

If the negative behaviour means that the individual's contribution is not acceptable and is disruptive then you must take action. Negative people can be quiet but they are usually angry about something; their negative behaviour is an easy way of expressing their anger. To deal with the problem it is necessary to find out what has made the person angry.

Causes of negative behaviour

There are many possible causes of negative behaviour which could include one or more of the following:

- a real or imagined slight from you or a colleague;
- a feeling of being put upon;
- a belief that the contribution made by the person is neither appreciated or rewarded properly in terms of pay or promotion;
- resentment at what was perceived to be unfair criticism from you or a colleague;
- anger directed at the company or you because what was considered to be a reasonable request was turned down, for example for leave or a transfer, or because of an unfair accusation.

Dealing with the problem

It is because there can be such a variety of real or imagined causes of negative behaviour that dealing with it becomes one of the most difficult tasks you have to undertake. If the action taken is crude or insensitive the negative behaviour will only be intensified. You might end up by having to invoke the disciplinary procedure, which should be your last resort.

In one sense, it is easier to deal with an actual example of negative behaviour. This can be handled on the spot. If the problem is one of general attitude rather than specific actions it is more difficult to cope with. Hard evidence may not be sufficiently available. When individuals are accused of being, for example, generally unenthusiastic or uncooperative, they can simply go into denial, and accuse you of being prejudiced. Their negative behaviour may be reinforced.

If you have to deal with this sort of problem it is best to deal with it as it is happening rather than waiting for a formal performance review.

The discussion should have three clear objectives:

1 To discuss the situation with individuals, the aim being if possible to get them to recognize for themselves that they are behaving negatively. If this cannot be achieved, then the object is to bring to the attention of individuals your belief that their behaviour is unacceptable in certain ways.

2 To establish the reasons for the individuals' negative behaviour so far as this is feasible.

3 To discuss and agree any actions individuals could take to behave more positively, or what you or the organization could do to remove the causes of the behaviour.

Discussing the problem

Start by asking generally how individuals feel about their work. Do they have any problems in carrying it out? Are they happy with the support they get from you or their colleagues? Are they satisfied that they are pulling their weight to the best of their ability?

You may find that this generalized start provides the basis for the next two stages – identifying the causes and remedies. It is best if individuals are encouraged to identify for themselves that there is a problem. But in many, if not the majority of cases, this is unlikely to happen. Individuals may not recognize that they are behaving negatively or will not be prepared to admit it.

You will then have to discuss the problem. You could say truthfully that you are concerned because they seem to be unhappy and you wish to know if they feel that you or the organization is treating them unfairly – you want to try and put things right. Give them time to say their piece and then provide a rational response, dealing with specific grievances. If they are not satisfied with your explanation you can say that they will be given the opportunity to discuss the problem with a more senior manager, thus indicating that you recognize that your judgement is not final.

If the response you get to these initial points does not bring out into the open the problem as you see it, then you have to explain how the individual's behaviour gives the impression of being negative. Be as specific as possible about the behaviour, bringing up actual instances. For example, a discussion could be based on the following questions: 'Do you recall yesterday's team meeting?', 'How did you think it went?', 'How helpful do you think you were in dealing with the problem?', 'Do you remember saying...?', 'How helpful do you think that remark was?', 'Would it surprise you to learn that I felt you had not been particularly helpful in the following ways...?'.

Of course, even if this careful approach is adopted, there will be occasions when individuals refuse to admit that there is anything wrong with their behaviour. If you reach this impasse, then you have no alternative but to spell out to them your perceptions of where they have gone wrong. But do this in a positive way: 'Then I think that it is only fair for me to point out to you that your contribution (to the meeting) would have been more helpful if you had...'.

Establishing causes

If the negative behaviour is because of a real or imagined grievance about what you or colleagues or the organization have done, then you have to get individuals to spell this out as precisely as possible. At this point, your job is to listen, not to judge. People can be just as angry about imaginary as real slights. You have to find out how they perceive the problem before you can deal with it.

It may emerge during the discussion that the problem has nothing to do with you or the company. It may be family troubles or worries about health or finance. If this is the case you can be sympathetic and may be able to suggest remedies in the form of counselling or practical advice from within or outside the organization.

If the perceived problem is you, colleagues or the organization try to get chapter and verse on what it is so that you are in a position to take remedial action or to explain the real facts of the case.

Taking remedial action

If the problem rests with the individual, the objective is, of course, to get them to recognize for themselves that corrective action is necessary and what they need to do about it – with your help as necessary. In this situation you might suggest counselling or recommend a source of advice. But be careful, you don't want to imply that there is something wrong with them. You should go no further than suggesting that individuals may find this helpful – they don't need it but they could benefit from it. You should be careful about offering counselling advice yourself. This is better done by professional counsellors.

If there is anything specific that the parties involved in the situation can do, then the line to take is that we can tackle this problem together: 'This is what I will do', 'This is what the company will do', 'What do you think you should do?' If there is no response to the last question, then this is the point where you have to spell out the action you think they need to take. Be as specific as possible and try to express your wishes as suggestions, not commands. A joint problem-solving approach is always best.

TEN APPROACHES TO MANAGING NEGATIVE BEHAVIOUR

1 Define the type of negative behaviour being exhibited. Make notes of examples.

2 Discuss the behaviour with the individual as soon as possible, aiming to get agreement about what it is and the impact it makes.

3 If agreement is not obtained, give actual examples of behaviour and explain why you believe them to be negative.

4 Discuss and so far as possible agree reasons for the negative behaviour including those attributed to the individual, yourself and the organization.

5 Discuss and agree possible remedies – actions on the part of the individual, yourself or the organization.

6 Monitor the actions taken and the results obtained.

7 If improvement is not achieved and the negative behaviour is significantly affecting the performance of the individual and the team, then invoke the disciplinary procedure.

8 Start with a verbal warning, indicting the ways in which behaviour must improve and give a timescale and offers of further support and help as required.

9 If there is no improvement, issue a formal warning, setting out as specifically as possible what must be achieved over a defined period of time, indicating the disciplinary action that could be taken.

10 If the negative behaviour persists and continues to seriously affect performance, take the disciplinary action.

Dealing with under-performers

You may possibly have someone who is under-performing in your team. If so, what can you do about it? Essentially, you have to spot that there is a problem, understand the cause of the problem, decide on a remedy and make the remedy work.

Poor performance can be the fault of the individual but it could arise because of poor leadership or problems in the system of work. In the case of an individual the reason may be that he or she:

- could not do it – ability;
- did not know how to do it – skill;
- would not do it – attitude;
- did not fully understand what was expected of them.

Inadequate leadership from managers can be the cause of poor performance from individuals. It is the manager's responsibility to specify the results expected and the levels of skill and competence required. As likely as not, when people do not understand what they have to do it is their manager who is to blame.

Performance can also be affected by the system of work. If this is badly planned and organized or does not function well individuals cannot be blamed for the poor performance that results. This is the fault of management and they must put it right.

If inadequate individual performance cannot be attributed to poor leadership or the system of work, these are the ten steps you can take to deal with under-performers.

TEN-STEP APPROACH TO MANAGING UNDER-PERFORMANCE

1 Identify the areas of under-performance – be specific.

2 Establish the causes of poor performance.

3 Agree on the action required.

4 Ensure that the necessary support (coaching, training, extra resources etc) is provided to ensure the action is successful.

5 Monitor progress and provide feedback.

6 Provide additional guidance as required.

7 If under-performance persists spell out precisely what improvements are required and issue an informal warning that if they are not achieved by a certain date disciplinary action may be taken.

8 If there is no improvement consider an alternative job.

9 If there is no alternative and there is still no improvement issue a written warning that disciplinary action in the shape of dismissal may be taken if the unacceptable level of performance continues.

10 If there is still no improvement take the action required to dismiss the employee.

Dealing with absenteeism

A frequent people problem you probably have to face is that of dealing with absenteeism. A recent survey by the Chartered Institute of Personnel and Development established that absence levels averaged 7.7 days per employee per year (CIPD, 2015). Your own organization should have figures which indicate average absence levels. If the levels in your department are below the average for the organization or in the absence of that information, below the national average, you should not be complacent – you should continue to monitor the absence of individuals to find out whose absence levels are above the average and why. If your department's absence figures are significantly higher than the norm you may have to take more direct action such as discussing with individuals whose absence rates are high the reasons for their absences, especially when they have been self-certificated. You may have to deal with recurrent short-term (one or two days) absence or longer-term sickness absence.

Recurrent short-term absence

Dealing with people who are repeatedly absent for short periods can be difficult to handle. This is because it may be hard to determine when occasional absence becomes a problem or whether it is justifiable, perhaps on medical grounds.

So what do you do about it? Many organizations provide guidelines to managers on the 'trigger points' for action (the amount of absence which needs to be investigated), perhaps based on analyses of the incidence of short-term absence and the level at which it is regarded as acceptable (software may exist to generate analyses and data which can be made available direct to managers through a self-service system). If there are no guidelines you can seek advice from an HR specialist, if one is available. In the absence of either of these sources of help and in particularly difficult cases, it may be advisable to recommend to higher management that advice is obtained from an employment law expert.

But this sort of guidance may not be obtainable and you may have to make up your own mind on when to do something and what to do. A day off every other month may not be too serious although if it happens regularly on a Monday (after weekends in

Prague, Barcelona etc?) or a Friday (before such weekends?) you may feel like having a word with the individual, not as a warning but just to let him or her know that you are aware of what is going on. There may be a medical or other acceptable explanation. Return-to-work interviews can provide valuable information. You see the individual and find out why the time was taken off, giving him or her ample opportunity to explain the absence.

In persistent cases of absenteeism you can hold an absence review meeting. Although this would be more comprehensive than a return-to-work interview it should not at this stage be presented as part of a disciplinary process. The meeting should be positive and constructive. If absence results from a health problem you can find out what the employee is doing about it and if necessary suggest that his or her doctor should be consulted. Or absences may be caused by problems facing a parent or a carer. In such cases you should be sympathetic but you can reasonably discuss with the individual what steps can be taken to reduce the problem or you might be able to agree on flexible working if that can be arranged. The aim is to get the employee to discuss as openly as possible any factors affecting their attendance and to agree any constructive steps.

If after holding an attendance review meeting and, it is to be hoped, agreeing the steps necessary to reduce absenteeism, short-term absence persists without a satisfactory explanation, then another meeting can be held which emphasizes the employee's responsibility for attending work. Depending on the circumstances (each case should be dealt with on its merits), at this meeting you can link any positive support with an indication that following the provision of support you expect absence levels to improve over a defined timescale (an improvement period). If this does not happen, the individual can expect more formal disciplinary action.

Dealing with long-term absence

Dealing with long-term absence can be difficult. The aim should be to facilitate the employee's return to work at the earliest reasonable point while recognizing that in extreme cases the person may not be able to come back. In that case they can fairly be dismissed for lack of capability as long as:

- the employee has been consulted at all stages;
- contact has been maintained with the employee – this is something you can usefully do as long as you do not appear to be pressing them to return to work before they are ready;
- appropriate medical advice has been sought from the employee's own doctor, but the employee's consent is needed and employees have the right to see the report, and it may be desirable to obtain a second opinion;
- all reasonable options for alternative employment have been reviewed as well any other means of facilitating a return to work.

The decision to dismiss should only be taken if these conditions are satisfied. It is a tricky one and you should seek advice before taking it, from HR, if available, or from an employment law expert.

Handling poor timekeeping

If you are faced with persistent lateness and your informal warnings to the individual concerned seem to have little effect, you may be forced to invoke the disciplinary procedure. If timekeeping does not improve this could go through the successive stages of a recorded oral warning, a written warning and a final written warning. If the final warning does not work, disciplinary action would have to be taken, and in serious cases this would mean dismissal.

Note that this raises the difficult question of time limits when you give a final warning that timekeeping must improve by a certain date, the improvement period. If it does improve by that date, and the slate is wiped clean, it might be assumed that the disciplinary procedure starts again from scratch if timekeeping deteriorates again. But it is in the nature of things that some people cannot sustain efforts to get to work on time for long, and deterioration often occurs. In these circumstances, do you have to keep on going through the warning cycles time after time? The answer ought to be no, and the best approach is to avoid stating a finite end date to a final warning period which implies a 'wipe the slate clean' approach. Instead, the warning should simply say that timekeeping performance will be reviewed on a stated date. If it has not improved, disciplinary action can be taken. If it has, no action will be taken, but the employee is warned that further deterioration will make him or her liable to disciplinary action which may well speed up the normal procedure, perhaps by only using the final warning stage and by reducing the elapsed time between the warning and the review date. There will come a time if poor timekeeping persists when you can say 'enough is enough' and initiate disciplinary action.

Handling challenging conversations

Many managers find it difficult to have conversations or hold meetings with individuals about performance issues. In advance these can look difficult and in practice they can be challenging if the manager wants to achieve desired changes or improvements in performance. They can be even more challenging in prospect if it is feared that unpleasantness may occur in the shape of lack of cooperation or outright hostility, or in practice when this happens in spite of efforts to prevent it. The following is a 12-point guide to handling challenging conversations.

1 Don't wait until a formal review meeting. Have a quiet word at the first sign that something is going wrong.

2 Get the facts in advance – what happened, when and why?

3 Plan the meeting on the basis of the facts and what is known about the individual. Define what is to be achieved.

4 Set the right tone from the start of the meeting – adopt a calm, measured, deliberate but friendly approach.

5 Begin the conversation by explaining the purpose of the meeting, indicating to the individual what the issue is and giving specific examples.

6 Focus on the issue and not the person.

7 Ask for an explanation. Ask unloaded questions to clarify the issues and explore them together.

8 Allow people to have their say and listen to them.

9 Keep an open mind and don't jump to conclusions.

10 Acknowledge the individual's position and any mitigating circumstances.

11 Ask the employee for proposals to resolve the situation, discuss the options and if possible agree on action by the individual, the manager or jointly.

12 If agreement cannot be reached, managers may have to define the way forward, with reasons – they are in charge!

EXERCISE 16.1

Challenging situation: What would you do?

The timekeeping of an individual member of your team has deteriorated badly over the last three weeks and is much worse than anyone else in your team. Here are some typical things you have to do or to deal with in this situation.

Select your preferred approach but note any other one which you think would be better than those listed below.

1 You want to speak to an individual about the problem.

You say:

(a) In my office – now!

(b) I have something I'd like to discuss with you that I think will help us work together more effectively.

(c) We need to talk about your timekeeping problem. Please come to see me at 4 pm.

(d) I would like a talk with you about your timekeeping. Let's grab a cup of coffee at 11 am this morning to chat.

2 You are starting the meeting.

You say:

(a) Is there any reason why your timekeeping hasn't been as good as it used to be?

(b) I have got your timekeeping record here and it's pretty poor. What are you going to do about it?

(c) As I told you earlier today, I would like to discuss your timekeeping with you. How do you think you compare with…?

(d) Thank you for coming. As you know, this meeting is about your timekeeping. Can we start by looking at your timekeeping records together?

3 The individual has agreed that there is a problem but gives what you think is an inadequate explanation for it.

You say:

(a) I am not sure that I really understand the problem. Could you tell me more about it?

(b) I think I appreciate the situation you're in but we must put our heads together and see what can be done about it.

(c) I cannot accept that as an adequate explanation. It's no excuse.

(d) I can understand your problem but how are you going to deal with it? The present situation cannot continue.

4 On being challenged by the time record and the unacceptability of the explanation, the individual relapses into a sullen silence.

You say:

(a) It's really no good behaving like this. We've got to move on.

(b) I don't know why you are not responding. What's the problem?

(c) We seem to have reached an impasse. I would like to reiterate the problem as I see it and I would be grateful if you would respond.

(d) I am not entirely happy with your explanation. Could you go through it again?

5 The individual goes into denial saying that he works very hard and often stays on, so why bother about being late now and again?

You say:

(a) The facts speak for themselves.

(b) Are you telling me that you are specially privileged and that you can start and finish any time you like?

(c) I appreciate that you work hard and conscientiously but do you think it would be possible for me to run this department if everyone turned up when they liked?

(d) Can we focus on the facts? You, like everyone else, are expected to turn up to work on time. Can you give me a really good reason for you being the exception?

6 The individual gets angry and starts shouting.

You say:

(a) I cannot tolerate this behaviour. We'll meet again when you are in a better mood.

(b) Calm down, dear!

(c) It seems to me that we need a cooling off period. Let's both think about today's meeting and reconvene tomorrow to discuss the situation.

(d) I appreciate that you are concerned about this situation but there is a problem and we need to discuss calmly how we can best deal with it.

SUMMARY POINTS

- If you manage people you have to manage people problems. They are bound to happen and you are the person on the spot who has to handle them. The basic approach you should use in tackling people problems is: get the facts, weigh and decide, take action, check results.

- Employees can be dismissed because they are not capable of doing the work or for misconduct. It is normal to go through a formal disciplinary procedure containing staged warnings but instant dismissal can be justified for gross misconduct (eg serious theft).

- If negative behaviour means that the individual's contribution is not acceptable and is disruptive then you must take action. Actual examples of negative behaviour can be handled on the spot. If the problem is one of general attitude it is best to deal with it as it arises rather than delaying the discussion to an annual performance review.

- In a case of persistent absenteeism start with a review meeting to discuss the causes and agree on what needs to be done to improve. Indicate that you expect absence levels to improve over a defined timescale (an improvement period). If this does not happen, the individual can expect more formal disciplinary action.

- If you are faced with persistent lateness and your informal warnings to the individual concerned seem to have little effect, you may be forced to invoke the disciplinary procedure. If timekeeping does not improve this could go through the successive stages of a recorded oral warning, a written warning and a final written warning. If the final warning does not work disciplinary action would have to be taken, and in serious cases this would mean dismissal.

- Many managers find it difficult to have conversations or hold meetings with individuals about performance issues. In advance these can look difficult and in practice they can be challenging if the manager wants to achieve desired changes or improvements in performance. A 12-point guide for holding such conversations is set out in the last section of the chapter.

Appendix
Notes on exercises

Exercise 1.1 Management qualities

The main qualities managers need are:

- the ability to make things happen;
- analytical, problem-solving and decision-making skills;
- proactivity (taking initiatives);
- creativity, social skills and abilities such as leadership, team working, customer care;
- relevant professional and technical knowledge;
- emotional resilience;
- communication skills;
- self-knowledge.

Exercise 2.1 Treating people with respect

- Deal with people as individuals with their own concerns rather than lumping everyone together and treating them the same.
- Recognize a person's qualities and honour their contribution, ensuring that they feel valued.
- Treat people with dignity and courtesy – no belittling in public, no bullying.
- Be polite at all times, even when issuing a reprimand or taking disciplinary action.
- Treat them as colleagues who will react responsibly to the right kind of encouragement, rather than as subordinates who are there to be ordered about.

- Listen to what people have to say. You don't have to agree with them all the time but if you disagree, do it politely.
- Recognize that people may have legitimate grievances and respond to them promptly, fully and sympathetically.
- Be firm with people when you have good reason to, but treat them justly and consistently.

Exercise 3.1 Assess your leadership skills

If you get:

- 35 points or more you are an exceptional leader and there's not much you need to do to improve.
- 30–34 points you are a good leader although there may be two or three areas in which you could do even better.
- 25–29 points you are a good enough leader but there are a number of areas in which you could usefully improve.
- 20–24 points you are a below-average leader and need to improve in a number of areas.
- 19 points or less you are a poor leader and there is a lot you need to do to improve.

Exercise 4.1 What do you know about motivation?

1 All the choices are correct but the one that provides the most comprehensive definition is (d).

2 The best choice is (a) – intrinsic motivation takes place when the work someone does is personally rewarding. (b) is incorrect; intrinsic motivation is about work, not personality. (c) is too sweeping; extrinsic motivation has a part to play alongside intrinsic motivation, especially in the form of recognizing achievements. (d) is correct as far as it goes but is insufficiently comprehensive.

3 The preferred choice is (b). As the term implies, extrinsic motivation consists of external rewards such as performance pay and praise. (a) has been shown to be incorrect by a number of research projects. (c) is only partially correct. There are other means such as recognition. (d) is likely but insufficiently specific as a definition.

4 (b) expresses clearly what motivation is about – seeking a goal the achievement of which will satisfy a need. (a) correctly indicates that highly motivated people are likely to perform well but motivation is best defined as the direction people take to achieve goals and not just the results they attain. (c) is clearly wrong. The use of rewards or punishments (the carrot and stick approach) is one way of trying to motivate people but it won't work in the longer term. (d) is wrong. Needs are not inevitably reassessed at this point in the motivation cycle. They could be, if new needs arise or the action fails to satisfy the original need, but if the goal is achieved the need will be satisfied and the behaviour is likely to be repeated the next time a similar need emerges. If the goal is not achieved the same action is less likely to be repeated.

5 The preferred choice is (c) because this expresses the essence of goal theory. (a) goes too far. The agreement of goals is very desirable but it is not the only way of motivating people. (c) also goes too far. Setting challenging goals will indeed motivate people but it is not the sole method. (d) rightly emphasizes the importance of feedback but this is only part of the goal-setting process.

6 The best choice is (a). This stresses the need for belief that their behaviour will produce a reward that they value. (b) is true but there is more to expectancy theory than that – it is not just about performance pay. (c) is incorrect – expectancy theory is not just about financial rewards. (d) is an inadequate choice – expectations of what?

7 Of the three choices, (a) is clearly wrong. It can be effective but other approaches can be equally or more effective for some people. Each of the other three choices has merit but, on balance, (b) is preferred because it expresses a fundamental truth about money and motivation which should be paramount – it should never be assumed that one method of motivation, eg performance-related pay, will be equally effective for everyone.

8 The preferred choice is (c) because it recognizes that there is more than one method of motivation. A combination of financial and non-financial rewards – what is called a 'total rewards' approach – can be the most powerful method of motivation. Both (a) and (d) are correct up to a point but neither tells the whole story. (b) is the carrot and stick approach which has been discredited as having only limited value in special circumstances. Moreover, it fails to convey to people that they are valued – it simply treats them like machines.

Exercise 5.1 Dealing with engagement problems

The outcome of the survey shows that there are serious problems with the ways in which people feel about their jobs and their attitude to their managers and supervisors.

A five-point plan for improving engagement levels could include:

1 Focus groups with employees to discuss the situation and obtain their views on what should be done.

2 A review of how work is organized and jobs designed in each department.

3 Intensive training for all managers on job design and individual coaching for those where there are particular problems as identified by the survey.

4 A leadership development programme for all managers and team leaders.

5 Intensive courses on coaching and developing people for all managers and team leaders.

Exercise 6.1 Case study: Work and organization design in Barchester Council

The main issue in this case is the organization of the different sections of the Housing Department into 'silos' and the consequent deskilling of work and poor morale. Service to customers is poor, as is productivity.

A radical change is needed. The organization should become customer-centred. One way of doing this is to set up groups, the members of which can deal with all aspects of a customer's housing needs in one place. Thus each group would cover housing advice, homeless people, registrations, allocations, temporary accommodation and income matters. Although initially group members would specialize in each area they could progressively learn to deal with other aspects of housing. Thus their jobs would be enriched, the groups could operate more flexibly and much better service would be provided for customers. It would have to be established how many groups were needed to deal with the normal flow of work. Customers when they arrived would be allocated to a group that had sufficient capacity to deal with them quickly.

Exercise 7.1 Investigating the quality of teamwork

A study of the survey results indicates that the problem is clearly one of leadership as shown by the responses to questions 5 and 1 and, possibly, question 4. An intensive leadership development course for team leaders is required, supplemented by individual coaching where this seems to be necessary. Some team-building training involving the whole teams would also be useful.

Exercise 8.1 How good a delegator are you?

Score your responses to each question as follows:

2 for often

1 for occasionally

0 for never

- If your score is 15 or more you have real problems as a delegator.
- A score of 10–14 means that you are not a bad delegator but that there is quite a lot of room for improvement.
- A score of 5–9 means that you are a pretty good delegator although there may be some areas where improvement would be helpful.
- A score of less than 5 means that you are a very good delegator.

Exercise 9.1 A case of job enrichment

The best way to enrich this job is to give Jane responsibility for more routine HR functions in headquarters, for example, recruiting junior staff and arranging for their induction to the company. She is intelligent and has the right kind of outgoing personality. She would have to be trained and fairly closely supervised to begin with but she is a quick learner.

Exercise 9.2 Preparing a basic role profile

The basic role profile derived from the role analysis is set out below.

Role title: Quality control technician.

Overall purpose of the role: To control the quality of the four products on the cooked meats product line.

Key result areas:

1 Conduct tests to establish the extent to which a range of food products meets quality standards.

2 Recommend to line manager actions to remedy quality problems identified by the tests.

3 Explain findings revealing serious issues to product development.

4 Prepare replies for customer services to send to customers who have complained about the quality of any item in the product range.

5 Prepare regular reports summarizing test results and findings.

6 Contribute to reviews of how quality standards can be improved.

Exercise 10.1 Conducting a performance review meeting

The main points to be covered are:

- where the individuals have got to;
- where they are going;
- how they are going to get there;
- what they know and can do;
- what they have learned or need to learn;
- what help or guidance they require.

Exercise 11.1 Selection interviewing skills

The following are the points that should be borne in mind when conducting a selection interview:

- put candidates at their ease;
- introduce the interview effectively;
- ascertain that they have prepared for the interview carefully;
- structure the interview logically;
- ask pertinent, clear and unambiguous questions;
- probe as necessary;
- avoid leading or multiple questions;
- allow the candidate to do much of the talking;
- keep control of the progress of the interview;
- maintain an easy and informal relationship;

- complete the interview effectively;
- obtain enough information about the candidate to enable you to make a confident assessment of their suitability for the job.

Exercise 12.1 What managers can do about learning and development

The things a manager can do to promote learning and development are to:

- understand the knowledge and skills required for effective performance in each of the jobs in his or her team;
- identify the learning and development needs of team members by observing and reviewing their performance to identify areas which need attention;
- use every contact with a team member to review performance, delegate work or give instructions as a learning opportunity for the individual concerned;
- pay particular attention to the induction of new members of the team to ensure that they know what to do and how to do it;
- provide coaching to develop specific skills;
- use systematic instruction methods to train individuals to carry out unfamiliar tasks.

Exercise 13.1 Managing performance-related pay

To make the best use of performance-related pay managers should:

1 Discuss with members of the team how the scheme will work and how they can benefit from it.
2 Ensure that performance targets are clear.
3 Ensure that performance targets are stretching but achievable.
4 Give guidance and help as necessary to enable individuals to achieve their targets.

5 Review performance jointly with individuals to assess the extent to which they have achieved their targets.

6 Assess and rate performance fairly, recognizing both good and good performance.

7 Explain to individuals the level of assessment they have been given and discuss with them how they can improve their ratings.

8 Be prepared to justify your assessments by reference to evidence of the level of performance achieved.

9 Understand and follow the guidelines issued by management on how the sum available for rewards should be distributed.

10 Explain to individuals the basis upon which their reward has been calculated.

Exercise 14.1 Managing change

To plan the change you will need to:

1 Work out the possible implications of the change for the department as a whole and its members.

2 Analyse the impact of the change on each member of your department.

3 Consider their possible reactions – immediate acceptance (unlikely), outright hostility (possible), concern about how it will affect them (very likely) or indifference (unlikely).

4 Consider how you are going to explain the change to the department as a whole, taking into account likely reactions.

5 Consider ways in which members of the department could be involved in planning and implementing the change (the new computer system may be a given, but the ways in which work will be reorganized could be the subject of discussion.

6 Prepare the communication and consider how any involvement could take place, eg assess the scope for flexibility in implementation.

7 Plan a timetable for communication, involvement and implementation.

Exercise 15.1 Managing conflict

You have a choice between:

- smoothing over differences;
- counselling;
- compromise;
- constructive confrontation;
- imposing a solution.

The best approach is constructive confrontation. You might be able to handle it yourself but an HR specialist (if there is one available) might be able to help. You have already rejected imposition but you may have to face the fact that when all else fails, that is what you may have to do.

Exercise 16.1 Challenging situation: What would you do?

1 Choice (a) is far too dictatorial; (b) is too vague; (c) is to be preferred, as it is a clear statement on what the meeting will be about – no surprises – and gives the employee time to collect his or her thoughts; (d) this leans too far into informality. It will be a formal meeting and the employee should be aware of this so as not to be taken by surprise.

2 Choice (a) is far too abrupt and is guaranteed to antagonize the individual; (b) is negative, abrupt and peremptory and would create a poor atmosphere from the start; (c) is generally a better approach but comparisons can only be invidious and does not address the real issue; (d) is better – it states clearly what the meeting is about and indicates that a joint problem-solving approach is being made based on evidence.

3 Choice (a) is potentially a helpful approach; (b) is better, as it assumes that the situation has been explored thoroughly and that a joint effort will be made to deal with it; (c) will only antagonize the individual and will mean that a reasonable solution is virtually

impossible; the first part of (d) appears to be reasonable although offering a joint problem-solving approach would be better. The second part is far too peremptory and would destroy any good the initial words may have done.

4 Choice (a) will only make matters worse; (b) is again a negative approach which will get the manager nowhere; (c) is positive and invites a problem-solving rather than an antagonistic approach; (d) is a reasonable approach but puts too much onus on the individual – managers are there to support their staff, not to leave them to sink or swim.

5 Choice (a) is entirely unconstructive and will only make a difficult situation worse; (b) is antagonistic and will mean that the meeting will become even more negative and unproductive; (c) sounds reasonable but a difficult customer may only think or even say 'that's your problem, not mine'; (d) ensures that the meeting focuses on the real issues based on factual evidence.

6 Choice (a) will only make matters worse now and in any future meeting; (b) is patronizing and counter-productive; (c) recognizes that in the heat of the moment little progress can be made but offers a future opportunity to reach a better outcome; (d) is fine up to a point, but things may have gone so far that they cannot be solved on the spot, so a cooling-off period might be best.

References

Adair, J (1973) *The Action-Centred Leader*, McGraw-Hill, London

CIPD (2015) Absence Management 2015 [online] http://www.cipd.co.uk/
hr-resources/survey-reports/absence-management-2015.aspx

Gray, D A (2010) Building quality into executive coaching, in *The Gower
Handbook of Leadership and Management Development*, ed J Gold,
R Thorpe and A Mumford, Gower, Farnham, pp 367–85

Heller, R (1972) *The Naked Manager*, Barrie & Jenkins, London

Herzberg, F (1966) *Work and the Nature of Man*, Staple Press, New York

Jaques, E (1961) *Equitable Payment*, Heinemann, London

Lawler, E E (2003) *Treat People Right*, Jossey-Bass, San Francisco

MacLeod, D and Clarke, N (2009) *Engaging for Success:
Enhancing performance through employee engagement* [online]
http://engageforsuccess.org/wp-content/uploads/2015/08/file52215.pdf

Maslow, A (1954) *Motivation and Personality*, Harper and Row,
New York

Pettigrew, A and Whipp, R (1991) *Managing Change for Competitive
Success*, Blackwell, Oxford

Pfeffer, J (1998) Six dangerous myths about pay, *Harvard Business
Review*, May/June

Pink, Daniel (2011) *Drive: The surprising truth about what motivates us*,
Riverhead Books, New York

Porter, L and Lawler, E E (1968) *Management Attitudes and Behaviour*,
Irwin-Dorsey, Homewood, IL

Tamkin, P, Pearson, G, Hirsh, W and Constable, S (2010) *Exceeding
Expectation: The principles of outstanding leadership*, The Work
Foundation, London

Index

Creating Success Series

The above titles are available from all good bookshops.

For further information on these and other Kogan Page titles, or to order online, visit the Kogan Page website at: **www.koganpage.com**.

CREATING SUCCESS

With over 1 million copies sold in over 30 languages, the Creating Success series covers 13 key skills and features bestselling authors Michael Armstrong and John Adair.

Dealing with Difficult People
Roy Lilley

How to Manage People
Michael Armstrong

Improve Your Communication Skills
Alan Barker

Taking Minutes of Meetings
Joanna Gutmann

How to Write a Business Plan
Brian Finch

How to Organize Yourself
John Caunt

Develop Your Leadership Skills
John Adair

How to Write Reports and Proposals
Patrick Forsyth

Decision Making and Problem Solving
John Adair

Develop Your Presentation Skills
Theo Theobald

Successful Project Management
Trevor L Young

Successful Time Management
Patrick Forsyth

How to Write a Marketing Plan
John Westwood

creating success
OVER 1 MILLION COPIES SOLD

@KPEmployability

www.koganpage.com/creating-success

KoganPage

creating
success

How to
Manage
People